How to Get Rich Through O P N

How to Get Rich Through O P N

Edwin M. and Selma G. Field

PARKER PUBLISHING COMPANY, INC.

West Nyack, NY

Library of Congress Cataloging in Publication Data

Field, Edwin M.
    How to get rich through OPN.

    Includes index.
    1. Business. 2. Success. I. Field, Selma G.,
joint author. II. Title.
HF5386.F414   650'.12   77-25513
ISBN 0-13-409508-1

HOW TO GET RICH THROUGH OPN

This book is about three little words and the big things they can do for you. When you begin to think in terms of OPN you will find thousands of profitable business opportunities. Successful businessmen and women have known the secret of these words since business began. In fact, no business can be successful without them. Yet, there is no magic involved in utilizing this secret. Man or woman, young or old, starting out or starting over, you can easily learn how to use these words to enrich your bank account and your lifestyle. In the pages which follow, you will discover how to use these words to make you as rich as you want to be.

Yes, indeed. You can get rich through OPN. These letters are simply an acronym for "other people's needs." It's no accident that when you try to pronounce OPN, it sounds like "open." Recognizing other people's needs literally opens the door to thousands of money making ventures. This book will show you how to identify these needs and how to analyze them for profit making potential. From the thousands of needs which exist all around you, you will learn how to select the ones best suited to your own needs.

Most important of all, this book will teach you, step-by-step, how to take advantage of these special opportunities to go into your own lucrative business, filling the needs of other people.

There are three especially nice aspects of the business of filling other people's needs. The first is that it can be done with limited capital, part-time or full time, from your own home or wherever you want to set up your business. The second is that when you really satisfy a need, you not only make money but you also get a particular satisfaction that goes beyond being just a cog in a wheel. You don't have to be a psychologist to recognize that people who receive satisfaction from their work are generally happier than those whose work is unrewarding. And, people who are happy in their work generally do better financially as well. The third aspect of OPN is that there are always needs to fill. In a crisis, no matter what its nature, those who are quick to see the new needs and to set about filling them can amass a fortune.

This, then, is your own "how-to-do-it" book. In Chapter 1 we will show you how to find profit filled needs, which you can use as the basis of your very own business.

Chapter 2 will introduce you to the ABC guide to assuring success in whatever business venture you undertake. The guide is a business counseling tool which you will be able to use over and over again, just as if you were coming to the office of the authors who are professional business counselors.

To help you determine just what needs you will want to use as the basis for your own business, each of the chapters, from 3 through 14 will discuss the opportunities which exist in various areas among different groups of people.

You will learn how to analyze the needs of business and industry and how to profitably fill these needs as an independent contractor. You will discover that you need not own a shop to find your profits in shopping centers. You will see how easy it is to combine business with pleasure as you meet the needs of hotels, resorts and convention centers. As you read the hundreds of success stories of others, you will develop the techniques of adapting their ideas in your own bailiwick.

The special needs of the very wealthy offer you distinct opportunities to become rich yourself. The man or woman who has "everything" can afford to develop extraordinary needs and to pay well for their fulfillment. The people who cater to the needs of the rich earn not only their own fortunes but, often, a degree of fame as well. If your interests and talents lead you in this direction, Chapter 4, will show you how to successfully serve this special clientele.

It is a truism that the busiest people, men and women, have a whole spectrum of needs which they will happily pay others to fill. Chapter 5 will help you analyze the needs of busy people and provide you with a dozen definite approaches to banking on these needs.

In other chapters, you will learn how to make money by cutting red tape; how to run an information service, a consulting firm, a lobbying business, a travel club, and hundreds of other businesses.

Before you finish this book, you will have at least a dozen ideas you will want to investigate for yourself. Chapter 14 will teach you how to investigate further, how to decide what to do, and most important, how to get started doing it.

One personal note. It took several months to write this book — that is, to get the words typed and printed. But, in a very real sense, this book has been in the writing for many years. The pr.nciple of making money by recognizing needs and filling them was the basis of our own successful business and has proven its worth for the hundreds of people whom we have provided with business counseling over the years.

Paul S. walked into our office one day about six years ago. A competent commercial artist who had worked for a major area firm, he had lost his job after fifteen years because of a corporate merger. He never wanted to work for anyone again, and who could blame him? But with four children approaching college, he certainly needed money. In a rural area, could Paul start a business of his own? We advised him to invest two weeks of his time investigating other people's needs. Do printing firms need free lance artists? Does the major mail-order firm need commercial art periodically for its catalogues? Is there a seasonal need for new billboard art? How many businesses in the area need a distinctive logo or symbol for their stationery and advertising? How many businesses in a hundred mile radius require periodic packaging designs or commercial exhibits?

When Paul came back after two weeks, he was exhilarated. "You know," he said, "there really is a tremendous need for this kind of service. Most firms need some art work but they don't need enough to keep a full-time man on salary. I'm going to open a studio and go into business. Thanks a lot."

"Now, wait a minute, Paul," we cautioned. "Let's sit down and talk about business."

"You've discovered a legitimate need which you can fill and which people will be happy to pay for. Now, let's analyze your needs. Do you need a studio or can you work at home?"

Paul thought for a moment. "You know," he said, "I'll be going out to other people's place of business. Nobody will be coming to mine. If I work at home, I don't need an extra phone; I can take an income tax deduction for the room I use; and I can work whenever I feel like it. Forget the studio. I'm going home to design my business cards."

Paul's children are now finished with college. The last time we saw him, he said: "You know, a lot of banks are merging and need new symbols. I'm branching out into the banking business."

He's become a healthy depositor, too. And, so will you when you begin to fill people's needs.

Edwin and Selma Field

Contents

5

How to Get Rich Through O P N

1

HOW TO FIND PROFIT-FILLED NEEDS

You carry the keys to discovery wherever you are. Since profit-filled needs exist or can be created almost everywhere, every need presents an opportunity. Your keys to unlocking these opportunities are your abilities to "see" the problems of people in different lifestyles and business situations. Simply stated these keys are:

Key 1: Dramatize
Key 2: Recognize
Key 3: Analyze

The ability to place yourself in someone else's shoes, mentally, and to play the role required by his or her lifestyle, will clue you

11

in to many needs. As you mentally dramatize a lifestyle, try to recognize and identify the special problems faced in that lifestyle.
This recognition opens the door to profitable opportunities half-
way. To unlock the door fully, each need has to be analyzed for
two special qualities: the inherent profits in the problem or the
need itself; and the profitability of the potential solutions.

THE MANY NEEDS YOU CAN FILL

If you can do any one thing reasonably well, there are countless opportunities for making money. If you are like most people,
there are many things you can do reasonably well and a few things
you can do especially well. This is true whether you are young or
older, male or female, educated or uneducated — and even if you
are physically handicapped. In addition to what you already can
do, there are hundreds of things you can learn to do if the motivation exists.

But, if you are like most people, you take your skills, abilities,
talents and interests so much for granted that you do not recognize them as money-makers in the market-place.

Debbie K. put herself through an Ivy League university by
recognizing that she could read reasonably well and use scissors.

Fred F. hobnobs with the wealthiest women in the world because he knows "where to buy anything wholesale."

Joanne Miley swept into business using her everyday housekeeping skills.

Pamela Moore Epstein turned her love of antiques into a career
as a lady auctioneer.

George Scota developed a business for his whole family because each brother and sister spoke four languages.

If you think about all of the businesses you know, you'll find
that many of them are based on simple, ordinary skills and knowledge. It's a worthwhile technique to analyze businesses this way.
It's even more helpful to recognize that these simple skills which
you possess could put you in the driver's seat of a luxurious foreign car or in possession of a six figure bankbook.

YOUR FIRST THREE STEPS

Most people don't realize how many skills they actually have. They are not always aware of the areas of specialized knowledge they possess. Nor can they readily identify the fields in which they are especially interested.

One way to unlock your opportunity potentials is to take a sheet of paper and fold it or rule it in thirds. (See Opportunities Potential Chart.)

Step 1: In column 1, list the things you believe you can do especially or reasonably well, your talents, special fields of interest, etc. Start from very basic things. Are you a good conversationalist? Or are you a listener? Reading? Penmanship? Typing? Mechanics? Gardening? Foreign Languages? Bread-baking? Clothes Shopping? Art or design? Teaching? Organizing? Gymnastics? Party-throwing?

Step 2: In column 2, list as many activities as possible which might utilize each of your skills. For example, a good conversationalist could be a host on a talk show; a lecturer for any group activity; an auctioneer; a telephone sales person; a fashion show commentator; a telephone pal to shut-ins, etc. An interest in reading might be utilized in a clipping service; in running book fairs for schools, organizations, and shopping centers; as a free-lance critic; by conducting a book-search service; by buying and selling rare books, etc. Those who speak foreign languages might list such activities as translating for courts, law enforcement agencies and other public bodies; writing ethnic columns for weekly newspapers; touring groups of foreign visitors; creating foreign language greeting cards; developing bi-lingual educational programs, etc.

Step 3: In column three, list those people, groups or businesses which might need the activities you have listed.

Opportunities Potential Chart

Skills, Talents, Knowledge and Special Interests	Activities or Careers	Needed by
House Plants	Raising plants for wholesale distribution.	Florists, specialty shops, department stores, schools, caterers, hotels, decorators.
	Raising plants for retail sale.	Homemakers, gift-givers, secretaries, executives, live-alones.
	Teaching "How to Grow..." classes.	Department stores, nurseries, adult ed and continuing ed departments at high schools and colleges; community centers; museums and galleries; individuals who might come to a class at home.
	Hybridizing house plants.	Nurserymen and florists.
	Photographing house plants.	Newspapers, magazines, book publishers, gift givers.
	Baby-sitting house plants.	Homemakers, offices, co-eds, vacationers, travel agents.
Listening	Phone companion.	Shut-ins, senior citizens, lonely people, guilt ridden families, social service agencies.

Opportunities Potential Chart, (Cont.)

Skills, Talents, Knowledge and Special Interests	Activities or Careers	Needed by
	Consumer representative.	Consumer industries, shopping centers, better business bureaus; people who don't know how to get the satisfaction they should from companies and stores providing services and products.
Reading	Literary critic. Literary agent.	Writers, publishers (books, magazines, newspapers).
	Book Fair Organizer.	Publishers, schools, PTA's, shopping centers, churches and other religious groups.
	Rare Book Seller.	Collectors, museums, special industries, colleges, libraries, etc.
	Book Search Service.	Other sellers, and all of the above, special interest groups.
	Clipping Service.	Businesses, celebrities, politicians and public figures, advertising and public relations agencies.

THE THREE PHASE OPN DIVINING ROD

Just as you can uncover opportunities by investigating your own skills and seeking needs to which to apply them, so also can you discover needs which can be profitably filled by adapting one or more of your talents. This can be accomplished easily by using the "divining rod" technique. This technique derives from the "dowser" who is said to find the best place to dig for water by using a willow branch as a divining rod. As the dowser walks slowly over the land, the rod is supposed to bend or twitch when water is under the surface. While modern scientists try to find out why this simple technique works, the folks who save money on their wells and get their cattle watered swear by the dowser.

You can test for OPN opportunities with your own three phase divining rod:

Phase 1: Every problem reflects one or more needs.

Phase 2: Every problem has one or more solutions.

Phase 3: Every solution represents a potential OPN opportunity.

HOW TO "IMAGINATE" PROFITABLE SOLUTIONS

We spoke previously about using dramatization as the first key to discovering opportunities. "If I were a rich man"...as Tevye dreams in *Fiddler on the Roof,* "would I need someone to count my money or to protect my possessions? How would I get to work in the morning — if I got to work at all? What obligations would I have and how would I fulfill them? How would I go about collecting rare antiques or modern art? Would I constantly be "taken" because I am rich? Would my family be easy marks because of the family jewels?"

As you put yourself in someone else's shoes and role-play his or her life, you will begin to recognize the problems apparent or under the surface in that life-style. You may want to confirm your feelings by doing some additional research, but your initial thoughts may very well put you on the track.

A world famous jewelry designer rose to prominence with a

successful large buiness enterprise because he sensed that if all wealthy women had lavish jewelry, much of it similar, the women would need something that might set them apart. He began designing individual "costume jewelry" pieces and showing them to jet-setters. While many of his items are expensive enough to fall into the luxury class for most of us, his clients consider them "fun" pieces which set them apart.

When we asked the son of one of America's wealthiest men why he suffered the physical strain and emotional abuse of a rough political campaign, he said, "There's a need to be somebody. There's a need to do something worthwhile, to leave a mark. There's a need to fulfill a family tradition of service."

How would you imagine a solution to those problems? More particularly, how would you imagine a *profitable* solution? If you use your imagination, you might ask yourself: What make's someone a somebody? By way of an answer, you might come up with: becoming a politician, becoming well known in social circles, being the subject of a book, becoming a leader in community volunteer projects, being the subject of columnists' patter, discovering a new drug or medical procedure or scientific process or industrial development, etc.

As you continue to imagine, you might begin to place yourself in the role with the solution to the problem emerging. How does one become the subject of a book or a leader in community projects or have his or her name associated with worthy developments in any field? Does one require a social secretary or a literary agent or a public relations campaign or an intermediary for grantsmanship?

Are there any of these needs you can fill? And, can you develop a good business doing it?

HOW TO ANALYZE A PROBLEM FOR PROFITS

In order to determine whether an OPN situation might be profitable, you must consider those elements a sales manager might evaluate if he were considering launching a new product. The first element is the size of the market. How many people have the same or a similar problem? If there are many people, then the market for a solution will be a large one and the potential of selling it will be good. The next major consideration is the income level or the economic status of the market. If millions of people need something but cannot afford to pay for it, they cannot ᴊe considered an OPN market. The degree to which people can anɑ will afford to pay to have a problem solved is an important element in the analysis. Another consideration if a need truly exists is whether someone else will or can be persuaded to pay to have the problem solved. For example, there are many senior citizens who cannot prepare their own meals and, therefore, have a dietary problem. A large number of these elderly folks cannot afford to patronize restaurants or have food sent in. Ordinarily, their problem would not be considered an OPN profit-opportunity. But, if a community organization or a government agency could be persuaded to meet the needs of these people, that organization or government agency might be a market for your services as a contractor for meal preparation or delivery.

In analyzing a problem for profits, you must think of the size of the market and the ability of the market (or some extension of the market) to pay for a solution. You must also think of the degree to which payment might go. A mass market that might afford only a few dollars for a service might not produce as much profits as a few individuals who could afford to pay thousands of dollars for a similar service if it were specially presented.

The hairdresser to the stars and celebrity jet-setters often receive ten to twenty times the fees of the beautician in the shopping center. In Las Vegas, those providing services to Arabian sheiks and oil magnates, and other wealthy foreign visitors, are reputed to receive tips of $50 and $100, many times what the average American tips for the same service.

The factors, then, in analyzing a problem for profits are: the size of the market; the ability to pay for a solution or to get someone to pay for a solution; and the degree to which a solution would be paid for. If these factors check out positively, then you can move to the next step.

HOW TO ANALYZE A SOLUTION FOR PROFITS

Once you have determined that a particular problem has a profit potential, you have to develop from your store of skills and talents, special interests and knowledge, a solution in the form of a product or service. Having developed such a solution, how can you determine if it will be profitable? The first step is to calculate as closely as possible what it will cost you to provide that product or service. The next step is to estimate what you can charge for your product or service to the market(s) you are considering. This is not a clear-cut or simple procedure. It may involve investigating what similar markets are paying for similar services or products. It may require a market test, asking a representative group of people what they might be willing to pay to have a certain problem solved. Or, it might be the result of your own feelings about a fair price. The third step is to calculate the potential profits from a *minimal* number of sales. The fourth and final step in the analysis is to decide for yourself whether this profit potential is worth it to you.

As you analyze any solution for profits, it is wise to keep in mind that while this solution may be a good one, it is probably not the only one. If you try the analysis on several possible solutions, you may find a wide range of profit potential differences. When you have reached a conclusion, you might find it worthwhile to review your problem and solution analysis with a trusted business advisor, a banker, attorney or accountant.

HOW TO DO MARKET RESEARCH
FOR PRACTICALLY NOTHING

Your closest public library can provide an impressive collection of market research data, available to you at the cost of your transportation to the building and the time it takes you to study it. What should you be looking for specifically? If you are interested in a particular industry, field of business, or area of activity, your first stop should be *The Reader's Guide to Periodical Literature*. This is a listing by subjects of articles which have appeared in magazines and newspapers in a specific time frame. When you have identified the subjects you are going to research, make a note of the listings which appear under that subject in the Reader's Guide. The librarian will usually be pleased to help you locate those of your listings which are in the library itself. In some instances, the librarian will be able to borrow the listings from another library or inter-library service. Among the libraries from which you might thus wind up borrowing books and periodicals are The Library of Congress, The State Library in your state, college and museum libraries, and libraries in adjoining areas.

In addition to using the public library for research, you can also secure vast quantities of research material at modest costs, often for nothing, by contacting the trade association in the field in which you are interested. You can locate the trade association headquarters by checking a directory of trade associations. One of the ones which is frequently up-dated is "The Encyclopedia of Associations," published by The Gale Research Company. The directories are rather expensive for one-shot use. You can often find them in libraries, in the offices of advertising and public relations agencies, and in municipal industrial development offices in your area. If you cannot locate one easily, you can usually find the name and headquarters of a trade association by asking someone in that specific trade or industry. For names of companies and their products, check *Thomas' Register* and *Standard and Poor's Register,* available in major libraries and banks.

Another source of free or low cost research material is the U.S. Government Printing Office, Washington D.C. 20402. In addition to providing bibliographies of material on particular subjects, the office issues periodic bulletins of available publications. You can get on the mailing list free by writing to the Superintendent of Documents.

Your daily newspaper will also provide you with an invaluable source of research material, at no extra cost if you read a newspaper anyhow. The trick of course lies in how you read the paper and what you are looking for.

MINING THE GOLD IN YOUR DAILY NEWSPAPER

Nearly every issue of your daily newspaper will contain a dozen or more leads to OPN opportunities. You just have to know what you are looking for. In the first place, you are looking for clues to problems. Your news stories continuously report the major problems facing large segments of the national and world population. Among the headlines which you may recall have appeared repeatedly are such problems as air and water pollution, drug abuse, world food shortages, population control, energy costs, health care costs, crime rates, etc. Because you know that these problems are of major proportions, you may assume that solutions will find ready markets. As you read through the paper you may not come up with a solution immediately, but you will want to clip the story or at least make a note of it.

Can you make money from these problems? Yes, you can. Every problem really represents a whole range of needs.

A nurse we know adapted the disposable hospital surgical mask for use by emphysema patients who are severely affected by chemical air pollution in industrial areas. A number of enterprising young men have revived interest in various devices to reduce gasoline consumption in autos. A friend has successfully developed a vegetarian cooking school promoted to alleviate food shortage and reduce health care costs. The increase of burglaries in suburban areas has led to a number of "house checking services" as well as an increase in the sales of various detection devices.

Your newspaper will not only report the problems. It will also report solutions other people have come up with. These should be noted just as the problems are. Can you adapt the solution to your own area? Can you improve upon the solution, making it more efficient or less costly? Does this solution stimulate your imagination to develop other marketable services or products?

While the headline stories, featuring the major problems and solutions, will be valuable to stimulate your thinking, the feature stories, particularly the biographical sketches of successful people will often produce more specific ideas. You will find these features in every section of the paper, from the women's page which covers food, family and fashion as well as clubs, organizations and society to the business pages which focus on industrial news. Even the comics can produce gold for those who know how to mine it.

Johnny B., an avid comic reader since his school days, picked five of the most popular comic strip characters, secured reproduction rights, and had a silk-screening shop print comic character tee shirts. He took the samples to prestigious golf clubs in the area, wound up with orders from the pro shops at the clubs and from the owner of a juvenile chain who played golf. He also sought out an advertising agent who was a member of one club and asked him to work out a direct mail and trade-advertising campaign. The campaign brought more orders than the small silk-screening shop could handle. As a result, Johnnie B. and the ad man formed a corporation to develop their own silk-screening plant. Using the signed orders as collateral, they were able to borrow sufficient funds from the bank to get started. Today, the advertising agency has become the secondary business and the comic strip characters have been joined by art nouveau creatures, sportsmen, product logos, etc.

The traditional source of opportunities in every newspaper is the classified section. It's time consuming to read the entire classified every day, but it's worthwhile to go through it frequently. You should be looking for job listings which run for comparatively long periods of time or which reappear frequently. These suggest that the employers might be better off by contracting for services. You should also be looking for articles for sale. Often these suggest OPN opportunities.

Two retired women in a Los Angeles suburb used to follow the articles for sale on a daily basis simply because they had nothing to do. One day over coffee they discussed the fact that several of their neighbors were advertising articles separately. Out of this discussion the women developed the idea of a commission sales flea market run on weekends. Today these two women have tripled their retirement income even though they take two months off each year to travel and see the world.

Norton K., a disabled veteran, capitalized on the classifieds by starting a "shopper's exchange." He contracts with a printer to publish this newsprint listing of classified ads twice a month. People pay $2 to have an ad listed once. The publication is distributed free at area grocery stores, antique shops, and diners. To get started, Norton contacted all of the area's antique dealers and as many collectors as he could find. He also phoned people whose ads ran in the local papers. Today, his listings come in by mail, each with a check. He calls his business "depression proof," noting that when economic conditions worsen there are more used items for sale, and more buyers for them.

Real estate listings can also provide good clues to other people's needs. When ads read "transferred, must sell home," what happens if the house is not sold before the owners move? When developers put up model homes, who decorates them? Who keeps them clean and attractive? Who checks to see that unlived in houses have not been broken into? Who checks to see that the electricity has not gone off, or the heat, that the burglar alarm is working, that the water pipes have not sprung a leak? Can a house on the market bring more money if it is freshly painted or cleverly decorated? These are just a few of the questions you might investigate from real estate listings.

Once you cultivate the questioning attitude, every single section of the newspaper can be fertile territory for prospecting. If you want to extend your scope, you might also ask friends and relatives to clip and save articles pertaining to subjects of special interest.

A FIFTY CENT KEY TO CONTINUOUS RICHES

As you accumulate clippings and ideas, you'll find that you develop a very special need of your own. How are you going to file the clippings and record the ideas so that they can be located months afterward in the middle of the night when inspiration finally glows? Everyone has to develop a filing system individually, because much of filing is judgmental. If you file your own clippings, chances are you will have some recollection of the judgment you used in selecting the subject under which each was filed. Even with the aid of your own memory, however, as time goes on and the file grows fatter, it's going to become difficult to determine whether that article on solar energy water heaters was filed under energy, water, household products or sun-power.

To help solve this problem, and also to serve as a quick reminder of projects under consideration, a fifty cent card file box is almost priceless. The three by five inch size is most convenient, but any size will do. A pack of file cards or pieces of paper cut to size, complete the process. Using this inexpensive device, you can file in whatever fashion you choose, but you will be able to keep a listing of where the article is on one or more file cards titled by subject and cross-indexed for other subjects which might be involved.

If you use the file box technique, a quick flip through can stimulate new ideas whenever you need them. It can serve as a reminder of projects you thought about before but never got off the ground, or it can fill in the last piece of a solution to a problem you've been puzzling out. You can also use the file box as a "tickler" system, by keeping a section for filing project ideas by date, and up-dating them every thirty days. Some people need this type of prod to keep them on track. Setting deadlines for accomplishing goals is a good way to achieve them.

ASKING QUESTIONS CAN MAKE YOU RICH

When Suzalee Sampsol watched her carpenter repair her kitchen cabinets, she noticed that he went up and down the ladder several times for various tools. "How many tools do you regularly use on an average job?" she asked. "Wouldn't it be more convenient to have them on a belt like the telephone linemen do?" The carpenter's affirmative response sent Suzalee to the craft shop to learn leather-work. Today, she sells carpenter's belts to lumber supply houses and fancy specialty shops catering to the "do-it-yourselfer."

On the commuter train one morning, Rubin Kranur sat next to the secretary of one of the community service clubs. "How do you manage to send out greeting cards to all your members for birthdays, anniversaries, etc.?" he asked. "My wife used to do it for me," the secretary replied, "but she just went back to school. It's become a real hassle to get the cards out and the meeting notices, newsletters, and special bulletins. I think the club is going to have to pay someone to do it." That innocent question, casually asked, led Ruby to a mailing service business which his wife ran until it became profitable enough for him to quit his job and expand the business.

While many questions innocently asked will lead you to OPN opportunities, there's nothing wrong with making it your business to ask questions about other peoples' businesses, hobbies, and special interests. "How do you go about getting started?" "Is it hard to find the help you need?" "What problems do you run into?" "How do you do it?" For the most part, people are flattered that you ask them. Many will go out of their way to be helpful in their answers. You shouldn't expect any real trade secrets, though sometimes you'll get those too, but you will get an insight into the problems and the solutions that may very well set you on the treasure train.

CREATING NEEDS TO BE FILLED

Years ago the average kitchen beckoned to the visitor with its smells redolent of the day's cooking. To many a toiler home from his labors, the odors wafting from the oven or burners were signs of a busy wife, a happy home, a favorite dinner. Somewhere along the line, room deodorizers, kitchen fans, and air changers were developed. Today it is a rare home or apartment that does not "need to be freshened" by one device or another.

Advertising has also created many other needs that people did not know they had. After all, there are only three basic material needs — food, clothing, and shelter. Other needs are emotional in nature, deriving their impetus from the ego. Services and products which appeal to the need to be loved, to be secure, to be unafraid, to be free from guilt, to be beautiful or handsome, to be recognized, to restore health or to live longer create special needs and special markets. While it is often more costly to tap the special markets because the needs have to be publicized, promoted, and advertised, these markets are often among the most lucrative of all.

Wherever you are and no matter what your interests are, there are needs waiting to be filled and needs waiting to be awakened. Your keys to discovering these needs, discussed in this chapter, can unlock hundreds of profitable doors for you.

2

AN ABC GUIDE TO OPN SUCCESS

HOW TO USE THE ABC GUIDE

This chapter will help you develop a successful business fulfilling the needs of other people. It is a brief distillation of the advice and experience of hundreds of people who have made it "big" on their own. It is also a springboard to new ideas of your own which will germinate from the thought seeds in this chapter. Therefore, it is suggested that you read this chapter with a notebook and pen or pencil at hand. Making notes as you read, and adding thoughts as they occur in the various categories will provide a continuing impetus for a successful venture.

ASSESSING YOUR MANY ASSETS AND ABILITIES

In the jargon of financial statements, your assets are all of your possessions — everything you own of tangible value. These assets might include a car or a home, a sewing machine or woodworking shop, a travel trailer or camper, or simply the furnishings of a studio apartment, some household equipment, a typewriter and a television set. The money you own — in cash, bank accounts and in investments — is also an asset, as is the cash value of any insurance policies you may own. If you add up the value of all of your possessions and subtract everything you owe — your outstanding loans, installment debts, mortgages and other obligations — your result is your net worth in dollars. For many people who have never submitted a financial statement to a bank, the "discovery" of this net worth is a surprise.

For the purpose of this assessment, however, the total net worth is tentatively less important than the various applications to which each asset can be put. A finished basement, for example, might be valued at several thousand dollars, but a classroom or a nursery school or a craft shop or a bookkeeping service facility which might occupy the same space has a far greater OPN asset potential.

In addition to the tangible assets and their tangible values plus the asset potentials which occur to you as you list your assets, you need to assess or appraise your intangible assets. These assets, which you cannot see or purchase, include the skills, talents, special interests and knowledge you listed in Chapter 1. To fully balance the net worth scale of intangible assets you should include those aspects of your personality and any other personal considerations which enhance the utilization of your skills. In place of obligations or liabilities, you might evaluate those conditions which might appear to limit or detract from your talents. It is important to consider these latter conditions carefully, for what might at first seem to be a minus can in many instances be turned into plus.

One of radio's most popular announcers could not seek an acting career because he was uncomfortable facing an audience or a camera.

Are you a "people" person or a "things" person? Have you lots of patience for intricate procedures or can't you wait to get a project over with? Can you tolerate a "service" relationship with clients? Are you a movie buff? Do you follow the soap operas intellectuals often scoff at?

At least one young women has capitalized on an interest in soap operas by publishing and selling a newsletter summarizing the stories of the most popular soap opera serials.

When we taught school and our students would ask "Why do we have to learn that?" we used to say "You never know when something you've learned or some experience you've had will become valuable to you. Sometimes when an important deal may depend on the impression you make, it might make all the difference if you can casually mention that the problem, like Gaul, is divided into three parts, or that a three foot circle will take less paint than a three foot square."

What you are trying to achieve in this assessment of your assets and abilities is a knowledge of yourself, what you can do, what you would like to do, what you would rather not do, and more specifically the tools you possess to help you accomplish your goals.

BUDGETING YOUR TIME AND MONEY

It is also important to determine how much of your time you are willing to spend and how much of your money you can afford to invest in your OPN business venture. Are you going to try to keep your job and develop your new business after hours and on weekends? Are you depending on your new venture to support you within a short length of time or can you afford to plow back income to expand your endeavors? Can and will members of your family give time to the new venture, answering phone calls, addressing envelopes or helping in any other way they might be required?

One Christmas week, Karel C., a steelworker, watched his co workers pay high prices for scraggly trees at a corner stall near the factory. That spring, after contacting the County Agricultural Agent, he persuaded his family to spend their weekends planting seedlings on his parents' scrubby acreage. Karel and others throughout the country have become Christmas tree barons,

earning enough from a few weeks of selling to carry them throughout the year.

Other families have developed profitable businesses catering
to the special needs of commercial decorators. While many farm
families struggled to make ends meet, one artistically inclined
mother persuaded her youngsters to grow the colorful indian corn
and gourds. These crops, which many farmers simply raise as an
afterthought, may not have as wide a market as food-crops, but
the financial return is far greater in the special needs market.

Years ago, when nylon stockings were replacing silks, rayons
and cottons, an unemployed young married man was nearly as
upset as his wife was whenever one stocking snagged just as she
was on her way to work. While he made the rounds looking for
work, he contacted a manufacturer and purchased a sample lot
of nylons. In the evenings, he and his wife packaged them three
to a pair. While the first triplets were sold by the wife to her co-
workers who liked the idea of a pair and a spare, the young man
sold them by direct mail to school teachers, building up a reorder
list which never tapered off until panty-hose became the rage.

After you've determined how much time and money you can
budget from your own and family assets, you might consider the
borrowing potential you have or can develop. If, for example,
you can secure firm orders for your new product or service, a
bank will generally give you a collateral loan. If special equipment is required, you can investigate the possibility of leasing
rather than purchasing outright. This has the advantage of con-
serving your capital at the outset, and also often renders a tax
benefit. If the leasing agreement includes the right to upgrade
equipment at moderate cost, this can be an important consideration in terms of minimizing future investment requirements. In
addition to collateral loans available through banks, these lending
institutions can be approached for straight business loans or
property mortgages to provide capital. Certain government agencies can also be sources of capital funding for small businesses. If
you cannot find out about these agencies from your banker or
accountant, you can write to your state legislator at his district
address if you know it or at the state capitol, or to your congressman or senator in Washington, D.C. These public servants whom

you have elected have staffs who can ferret out information for you and direct you to the agencies which might be applicable. They can provide you with valuable contacts.

CLASSIFYING YOUR SCOPE OF CONTACTS

We have said that everything you learn or experience can be important to you at some time. Nevertheless, the old adage, "It's not what you know, but who you know..." is not without an element of truth. People with many diverse contacts in important places appear to have a head-start. They seem to be in a position to secure early information on emerging needs, and they are often given an inside track position in opportunities to fill the needs.

Whom do you know? Before you answer, "Nobody important," try compiling a list of your contacts. Just as you were able to compile an impressive number of your skills by thinking about them in different ways, you can produce a surprising number of contacts if you spend some time at it.

How about your former schoolmates? What are they doing now? What organization do you belong to? What positions do your co-members hold in the community? Did you ever participate in a political campaign or a fund-raising effort? Who worked with you? What business people do you do business with? Your doctor, lawyer, accountant? The parents of your children's friends? Your social worker or unemployment counselor or the heads of any social service organization you might have had contact with? Your minister or rabbi? Your present or former co-workers? The relatives of relatives? The superintendent in your apartment building. Depending on what you want to accomplish, contacts can be almost anyone you know or can find a way of knowing.

When Elmer S., a supermarket clerk who lived with his mother in a once fashionable apartment building, recognized that his mother's friends were afraid to go out to grocery-shop, he sensed an opportunity. He envisioned running a buying and delivery service that would earn enough to move his mother to a house in the country. Aside from the half-dozen or so of his mother's friends in the neighborhood, Elmer had no real contacts, even in his own apartment building. But, he knew the super who gave him the names of all the apartment dwellers in the building and the names of the supers in adjoining apartment houses. After Elmer had arranged for a quantity purchase discount with the manager of his market, he canvassed the apartments, explained his projected service and announced that he would pass along savings over his expenses. He set a $2.50 service charge per delivery, reasonable enough since many of the women had been using taxis to help bring home their packages.

The response was good enough for Elmer to give up his job at the supermarket. He and his mother never did move to the country though. Mother was kept busy answering the phone taking grocery-pick-up orders which were filled twice a week from a panel truck Elmer purchased on installments. In the process of developing this service, a new need emerged. People needed all sorts of things picked up — and delivered — pets from the vet, plants from friends and relatives, an appliance from the discount shop, etc. Elmer set his special services rates on the basis of time and distance involved, averaging approximately $6.00 an hour and twenty cents a mile. While his mother thought these prices were somewhat steep, the special orders kept coming in. The special orders had a bonus for Elmer. As he drove his panel truck all over the city, an entire new clientele developed from seeing the mobile billboard "ELMER'S DEPENDABLE DELIVERY AND PICK-UP SERVICE. IF YOU NEED IT WE'LL GET IT TO YOU."

You can be assured that the super in Elmer's building has received a generous Christmas present every year. He turned out to be a most important contact.

DEVELOPING CONTACTS FOR PROFITS

After you've compiled the list of contacts you've already made, it's a good idea to add a classification for contacts you can easily make. These include your public officials, local, state, and federal. Many of them are surprisingly accessible, particularly if they must run for office. If you wish to cultivate these people as firm contacts about the easiest way is to volunteer to serve in their campaign, stuffing envelopes, making phone calls, working on statistical reports, arranging rallies, or whatever might be needed for periods of time you might have available. Since many candidates do not run their own campaigns, it is a contact investment to find some way to let the candidate know that you are working for him or for her. The opportunity to do this is frequently available if you're not terribly shy or retiring.

You can always make contact with people who have a mutuality of interest in one of your undertakings. If you are going to provide the answer to a problem for someone, the chances are that individual will appreciate your contact. This generally applies to the largest corporate officers as well as to the man on the corner.

The important lesson to learn in developing contacts is that the world does not destruct simply because you are rebuffed once or twice. If you ask someone to do something for you and it is not done, are you really any worse off than you were before you asked. If, however, you are dealing with patentable products or unique applications of a product or service which might be taken from you by an unscrupulous contact, it might be wise to discuss means of protecting your ideas before you make your contacts.

ENERGIZING FOR A FAST START

You have assessed your assets and abilities, budgeted your time and money and classified your contacts, developing a strategy for making new ones where necessary. These exercises are essentially energizing or fueling you for a successful start. The best solution to any problem can't make any profits for you unless you are ready to move on it. You can't be successful unless you get started. While it makes sense to cautiously analyze all of the elements of a potentially good business proposition, you have to be ready and willing to try it once you are convinced that you can analyze no further. You may want to try it in a test market or in some limited fashion. You may want to spread the risk — if you see a risk — by involving other people. But, one way or another, unless you try it at all, you can be sure that someone else will get around to it before you do. As needs arise, many people apply themselves to filling them because that is the nature of business.

The fact that many come up with the same answers does not necessarily mean that they are stealing each other's ideas. It may simply be a result of the same thought process. However, all other variables being equal, those who come out with a new product or service first in their area generally have a decided advantage.

We've spoken about setting deadlines for yourself as an energizing technique. If you set yourself target dates for the achievement of each phase of your pre-business planning, you'll move forward more rapidly even if you don't always meet the deadline. You know best the techniques which motivate you to action. As you become consciously aware of these energizers and employ them to keep you moving toward your goal, you'll be that much closer to getting into business for yourself.

FEELING YOUR WAY INTO A BIG BUSINESS

You may have lots of time and sufficient capital to go into a business of your own. You may have developed what you and your advisors believe is a promising, profitable solution to a recognized need. But, you may be afraid to take the plunge until you have verified for yourself that what you believe to be true will actually prove to be true.

The solution is to feel your way into a big business. The way to do this — as big business does when it plans to introduce a new product — is to test market your product or service. There are numerous books and trade journals on marketing, direct mail, and advertising which discuss methods of test marketing. Essentially, the principles are the same. A small but representative sample of the potential market is approached for its reaction to the new product or service.

If you are going to be selling by direct mail to a specific market, you might try a mailing of 250 instead of 1,000 or 10,000. If you are planning to sell by advertising, you might use several small ads instead of an advertising campaign. Many services can best be sold by personal contact. In this instance it's necessary to actually try to sell the service to a fair sampling of your market.

Another aspect of "feeling your way" is to be cautious about heavy initial investment. If you are going to be selling a product of your own creation or manufacture, you should have a number of perfect samples and you should be absolutely sure that you have a ready source of necessary raw materials. As long as the raw materials will be available within a short period of time from someone else's inventory, you don't really have to invest in large quantities until you know you need them. In terms of your acquisition of expensive equipment, you may want to consider short term rental, or leasing or you may want to investigate shared time on someone else's equipment. Sometimes if the equipment is very costly, it pays to have your product manufactured by someone else — or to find an existing product which can be adapted to your purpose.

Julie and Michael S. wanted to commercialize the hand-turned wooden peg toys they had made for their young son, but they were not prepared to invest in power equipment. They found a furniture factory which *discarded* odds and ends of genuine walnut stock. The wood remnants were the pieces left after furniture legs were turned, cut and trimmed to size. The couple hand-sanded the raw edges on a sample lot, packed them in clear plastic bags, and gave them to nursery schools. They asked the schools to let them know how the youngsters reacted to the odd shaped blocks. When the favorable responses came in, Julie and Michael took them and a batch of new samples to the toy buyer of an exclusive department store. Only after several purchase commitments were made did the couple secure their power equipment — second-hand from a furniture factory.

Feeling your way into a business may mean starting small. But, if you really have a product or a service which is needed you can promote it to a major place in the business marketplace.

GENERATING INTEREST IN YOUR PRODUCT OR SERVICE

Elmer S. used several techniques to generate interest in his shopping and delivery service. The first was "word-of-mouth" — his own, his mother's, the super's and his customers'. The second was his mobile message on his panel truck.

You might adapt these techniques, or you might use a host of others. The important thing is to use some means to attract attention and business. Unless you are highly visible in a high traffic area, just being in business is not enough to bring customers to your door.

Within the confines of your budget you might consider: direct mail promotion (letters, postcards, brochures and gimmicks); advertising (classified or display in daily or weekly newspapers, organization newsletters, trade journals and magazines; or radio and television commercials; billboards and signs); and flyers, leaflets or posters.

You might also generate interest by using public relations techniques such as publicity and promotion, special events and tie-ins. Karel C. used this approach. He contacted the business and family editors of newspapers in a hundred-mile radius and invited them and their families to a Christmas party in July. The picnic-style party attracted a dozen newspaper people, each of whom eventually wrote a story about the Christmas tree farm.

HELPING YOURSELF TO LOW COST PROMOTION

If Karel had bought the space the newspapers used for the stories, he would have paid hefty advertising bills. Instead the publicity generated by his Christmas in July party cost him only the expenses of a hot-dog, hamburger, and watermelon picnic for thirty people, and the outlay for invitations and postage. As a result of the stories which appeared in various papers, Karel was invited to a television talk show which created further interest.

If your product or service is unusual or different from most available, or if something about you or the way you are approaching your market is different, you can achieve this free publicity and exposure. A letter, as brief as possible, describing the interesting facets of your business, should be prepared as a stock form. You can then individualize this form letter to make it applicable to newspaper people in various departments of the area papers, to program directors of radio and television stations, and to program chairmen of various clubs and organizations. These letters should be followed by phone calls within a week. If there is no immediate interest, ask to be considered in the future. Most writers and directors keep a stand-by file for slack periods and may call you long after you've forgotten the initial contact.

You can also write your own news release or feature stories about your new business. The first article should be an announcement of the opening of a business or the establishment of a service. This announcement should be written in the third person in a fashion something like this:

> *Your Service Established*
>
> Your City: An announcement of a service to meet the needs of *your market,* was made this week by *your name, business address, Mr. or Mrs, or Miss Your name* said that the service will cater to *the various groups of people who need the services you offer.*

Succeeding paragraphs of the news release should repeat the trade name you will be doing business under; the geographic area you propose to cover; something about your background which will lend credibility to your ability to deliver the service; and more about the needs your service will fill.

The release should be written as though someone else were writing about you. You can learn more about the format of a news release by following the business pages of area newspapers. When the release has been written, it should be neatly typed and photocopied for distribution to newspapers, or it can be mimeographed or duplicated. If photographs are available, they can be descriptively captioned and forwarded with the release.

Releases can also be written about special events, open houses, demonstrations, business growth, etc. In some instances, newspaper editors will use your release as a basis for an article. In others, a reporter might be assigned to follow-up for a human interest story. It is good practice to include a notation "For further information please contact..." with your name and phone number. The same release can be sent to all media including trade journals in your field.

Other low cost exposures can be arranged by contacting the newsletter editor for your church, synagogue or service clubs, or your fraternal organizations. In addition, flyers, posters, or announcements can be placed in supermarkets, shopping centers and organization centers. Schools, colleges and some public buildings also offer bulletin boards for announcements. In most instances, permission for posting should be requested, as a matter of courtesy and to comply with any requirements.

IMPRESSING THE PEOPLE YOU NEED FOR SUCCESS

There are two ways to leave a marked impression on people. One is to be a personable eccentric. The other is to be outstandingly competent and knowledgeable in your field. Fortunately both eccentricity and competence can be developed. The latter is simply a matter of knowing as much as possible about the field you are in and doing a workmanlike job on every project, demonstrating a sense of pride in yourself and your efforts. The smallest customer may lead to the largest account. The air of competence you display may convince an investor or a banker to back you. To display this you have to believe in yourself, be convinced that you have something to offer. This is not to come on strongly egocentric. In fact it is important to learn how to play down the "I", to nod your head in agreement as an attentive listener, and to raise those points which you know your audierc⌄ will agree with.

Helping someone else feel important raises your own "recallability." Coming to an appointment fully prepared with the tools you require or all the information you need also impresses people with your businesslike approach. While neatness, in appearance and on the job, is important, many people are impressed by "true-to-their image" characterization. People remember the artist with the handlebar mustache or the artiste with the patchwork smock.

You don't have to be weird to be considered eccentric, you just have to be distinctive in some way. A public relations man we know is considered eccentric because he is a vegetarian and does not imbibe alcoholic beverages. A dressmaker always wears one article of yellow, a scarf or fresh rose, or a broach. A distinguished plastic surgeon wears white tennis shoes year round, even with his tuxedo. These people leave a lasting impression on people they meet because they can be recalled with clarity. Combining this distinctive impression with one of competence is an art worth cultivating.

JUDGING YOUR COSTS

If you are to appear businesslike and to conduct a profitable business, it is essential to know preceisely how much your product or service costs you. Costing out a product you manufacture requires an analysis of the costs of raw materials, packaging materials if any, and labor, your own and that of others you employ. Other factors which enter into costs are fixed overhead expenses such as rent, heat, light, telephone, etc.; depreciation of equipment (or leasing costs); distribution costs, if any; advertising and sales promotion. While accuracy is possible in cost analysis accounting, it may be difficult to evaluate exactly what fractional part of fixed expenses can be fairly attributed to each item produced. If this is the case, it is better to overestimate than to err in the opposite direction.

As you calculate the costs initially, you might keep in mind that generally as production increases, the cost per unit decreases since smaller portions of the fixed expenses can be attributed to each item. Purchasing raw materials in larger quantities may also reduce costs, as might more efficient labor utilization.

Labor is the chief cost ingredient of a service business, though fixed expenses can contribute to service costs. If your own labor is the chief cost factor you can set a value on that labor in a number of ways. One is to establish what you might be earning if you were working for someone else. Another way is to set your own labor cost at what you would be or are paying for labor. Neither of these ways adequately reimburse you for your administrative and managerial responsibilities. The remuneration for these should come out of your profits. They may be established as part of your cost or as part of your mark-up.

Many people who are starting a business of their own initially undervalue the costs of their own time and labor, considering it part of their investment in their future. There's nothing wrong with this attitude as long as it is consciously recognized and taken into consideration when prices are established.

In a service business which utilizes equipment and products, these costs must be analyzed in addition to the labor. Once again it is wiser to judge costs on the high side rather than the low, to establish a cushion for unexpected expenses.

Cost estimates should be calculated and recalculated frequently. As experience data from your operation periodically becomes available, cost judgments should be refined.

KEEPING ACCURATE RECORDS

No matter how small your business is, accounting records are a management tool essential to success. It is, of course, necessary to keep records for tax purposes. It is as important to keep records which you can analyze and evaluate for trends which you can influence or control.

The system you use is not as significant as the accuracy and consistency of systematically recording every single business transaction in its proper category. These categories include:

1. assets
2. liabilities
3. income
4. expenses

The tendency in early stages of a business is to believe that large transactions can be remembered and small ones are too trivial. Often, there are so many business activities that bookkeeping is put off until "there's more time." Both of these attitudes can contribute to business failure.

If time is at a premium, or if you are going to have someone else do your bookkeeping, it is helpful to keep your own daily business diary. This can be a pocket-sized notebook or a daily sheet on a clipboard. It only takes a minute to make a note of each purchase and sale as you make it and to jot down any out-of-pocket cash expenses you incur for supplies, business entertainment, business travel, etc.

Cash expenses in some businesses can reach comparatively high levels and become significant tax deductions if adequate substantiating records are kept. A check issued periodically for "petty cash" can help keep an accounting of cash expenditures. Another helpful practice for better monetary control is to deposit all income to a single checking account and to make all payments or withdrawals by check.

Your business records will enable you or your accountant to prepare a balance sheet, or statement of net worth, by comparing your assets and liabilities; and a profit and loss statement, or statement of income and expenses. Bankers and other potential investors will look to these statements for the financial status of your business and the direction it has taken.

LASSOING BIG CLIENTS

Shana and Lou W. gave up college art teaching to work independently as potters. A small shop in their home produced a modest income, augmented occasionally by participation in arts and crafts shows. At one show in a major shopping center, Shana approached a buyer for one of the large department stores.

"Do you think these would sell in your boutique?" she asked.

"If we could work out a satisfactory wholesale price, I'd try a dozen planters," the buyer replied.

That night, Shana recounted the big sale to Lou. "It was so easy," she said. "All I had to do was ask."

You will often surprise yourself with all of the business you can get simply by asking. You can ask for business by advertising, by mail, or by phone, but the best way to lasso a really big account is by personal solicitation. If you are filling a genuine need, it's just as easy to solicit big orders or contracts as small ones. What's important here is the attitude you develop. As long as you remember that when someone turns you down you're no worse off than before you asked, you'll find that more people will accept than will refuse. If you're talking about really big orders or contracts you really don't need many.

If you are prepared, for example, to provide meals for senior citizens, you might approach nursing homes for food service contracts as well as servicing individual clients at home.

If you are opening a gift buying service you might seek mass orders from personnel officers and sales promotion directors of major corporations as well as from individuals.

If you are running a party-catering service you might consider soliciting business from the more socially prominent and the more affluent who would be most likely to pay more for your services than other groups and would probably need your help more often.

Many people have built big businesses based on many, many small sales. There is nothing wrong with this approach. But, a big client can help a business grow bigger faster and can add the prestige which attracts other customers large and small.

MULTIPLYING PROFITS THROUGH FRANCHISES

If you can develop a systematic approach to filling a particular need with a service or product, you may find that your successful business can be duplicated anywhere the need exists. You could open branches of your own and employ people to run them for you. Many people have taken this route to big business. The obvious drawbacks are that a capital investment is required for each new branch and competent, trustworthy managerial personnel is not always easy to come by, particularly with absentee management.

Another method of expanding your own income is by franchising — by giving others in selected areas the right to duplicate your business for a fee. Both product and service businesses have been successfully franchised. There are many instances in which the franchise operation has produced far greater income than the prototype on which the franchise is based.

If you believe that you have developed a successful business which can be duplicated in many areas, franchising may bring you more money than you ever dreamed of having. You could pursue the franchise route on your own, but it requires some specialized legal knowledge to protect your interests, and some specialized marketing and promotional expertise to sell your franchises in a highly competitive market. Before seeking the legal and marketing help you may need, it would be a good idea to read a number of current books on franchising and to check with your accountant and attorney for general advice on how to proceed.

NEGOTIATING CONTRACTS FOR CONTINUOUS INCOME

A sheaf of signed contracts for your services or products is an indication of the forward direction of your business. While such contracts are not generally negotiable, many contracts can be assigned or used as collateral, and in the sale of a business, such contracts enhance the value.

A contract is simply a legally enforceable agreement between two (or more) parties in which one agrees to do something in return for consideration by the other. Under some circumstances a binding contract may be made orally. You can better protect your interests by a carefully drawn contract in which your obligations to provide services or products are specifically spelled out along with the terms by which you will be paid.

When you ask your attorney to prepare a contract form, you should be prepared to discuss the specific aspects of your business which make it different from others with which he or she might have dealt. An attorney can be expected to be an expert in the law, but is not necessarily aware of every ramification of every business or service.

Since a contract binds you as well as your customer, special thought should be given to the length of time it will run, the options for termination or renewals, and the arrangements for changes, if any, in price. In an inflationary period, a long term contract at a fixed price may contribute to a disaster. In periods of relative stability long term contracts, while limiting flexibility, contribute to the security of the business.

Consideration should also be given to the renewal clause(s). A contract which is automatically renewed, unless some step is taken to terminate it, is more likely to provide greater security for you than one which must be physically renewed periodically.

OPERATING FROM LOW COST LOCATIONS

The challenge to management is to maximize income while minimizing costs. One of the areas in which you can exercise cost control is the selection of your business location. The difference in rents between prime locations and out of the way sites can amount to several thousand dollars a year. Even greater actual savings and tax benefits can be achieved if you can operate your business from your own home or apartment.

While there are some businesses which benefit to a degree from having a prestigious address and plush interiors, most businesses which fill a genuine need do not require prime locations and concomitant high rentals. Businesses which perform services at the customer's home, office, or plant require little more than space to store necessary equipment, bookkeeping and secretarial space, and a telephone. If zoning ordinances and dwelling restrictions permit, this type of service business can be conducted from your home. In many instances it is economically feasible to rent or purchase a larger home to accommodate both your living and business needs. The rental you would pay for outside facilities plus the tax benefits resulting from business use of residential property can often totally offset the costs of the larger residence.

Even if you cannot conduct your business from your home, you do not have to select high rental areas for your business unless there are compelling reasons to do so. People tend to seek out firms which meet their needs. If, however, for reasons of proximity to your market or for prestige purposes which can raise the selling price of your service or product you believe you must be in a high rental area, you might investigate the possibility of sharing space with professionals, or other business people utilizing lofts or other space above or below the main floor of a building.

Maintaining fixed expenses at the lowest possible level consistent with business objectives is a hallmark of successful businesses. If you can save $1,000 a year or more on rent without affecting your gross volume, you can add that much to your profits each year.

PLANNING AND PRICING FOR PROFIT TAKING

Profits are the difference between your income from sales or fees for service and your expenses. While it is vital to keep your expenses as low as possible and to generate demand for your services or products, it is equally important to establish your pricing structure so that the results of your efforts are worthwhile. You can price yourself out of business by selling too high — in which case you will lose your market, or by selling too low — in which case you will be spinning your wheels.

There are several ways to establish prices for profits. The first is to identify your actual costs per product or service unit and to add mark-up which will give you an adequate profit including compensation for your own or family labor. This pricing structure can be tested for consumer response in a sample market. A more than adequate response might indicate that prices could be inched upward without reducing sales. A smaller response than anticipated should be evaluated not only for a pricing problem, but also for a marketing or product problem.

Another way to establish prices is to check the competition, if any, or the charges of similar businesses in other areas. This can be accomplished generally by a phone call on the pretense that you or the caller is an interested potential customer; or by having a friend write for prices and available literature.

Arts and crafts often are priced differently for various markets. If you are producing for boutiques, specialty departments or stores, or museum shops, you must consider that your selling price is a wholesale price to which a profit margin is added by the retailer. If you sell to retail markets, it is important to reserve the right to sell your own products in your own shop if you desire to do so.

The pricing of "originals" is often a response to the demand or a reflection of what the traffic will bear. Often a gallery or shop owner will give you an idea of a price range for your original work even if he or she is not prepared to handle your work. A good publicity and promotion program which creates a demand for your name-signed originals can often raise their prices tenfold or more.

Unique or unusual services to affluent markets can also be priced on the "traffic" principle. If you can negotiate personally, you can often frankly admit "I don't know precisely how much to charge for this. What do you think is fair?" Or you might say "My usual fee is X dollars," quoting a higher figure than you anticipate receiving, "But, I'm prepared to negotiate."

These approaches may seem un-businesslike, but they are not. Some attorneys charge $25 an hour for their time and others charge several hundred, depending on their clientele. The same is true of other professionals.

Whatever approach you use to pricing, a periodic review is necessary to maximize profits.

QUESTIONS TO ASK YOURSELF EVERY DAY

1. Can I improve my product or service for greater profits?
2. Can I expand my market for greater profits?
3. Can I add new lines or services for greater profits?
4. Can I reduce costs and expenses for greater profits?

REACTING TO CHANGE FOR GREATER PROFITS

Sam and Jack S. started a feed and grain business in the 1920's, only to find the horse and buggy being replaced by the automobile. Undaunted, they added a gasoline storage tank and pump, then another, and still another. Because the cars kept coming, there was a need for repair parts and tires which were also added to the inventories.

Bert S. had developed a successful floor sanding and finishing business when he noted the trend of builders using unfinished sub-flooring covered with carpeting or tiles. Contacting the builders for whom he had previously worked, Bert added carpet and other floorcovering installation to his services.

Changing needs may close out one set of opportunities, but they always offer new ones. The ability to recognize change and to react to it positively and quickly is a definite determinant of long term success. Fortunately, it is an ability which can be developed if you continue to use the rules in Chapter 1.

SELLING YOURSELF WITHOUT EMBARRASSMENT

When you are legitimately filling needs for people or industry you are performing a valuable service for them. You are doing something which they want to have done, but which they cannot or will not do for themselves. Your products or services are important and you are important.

A lady lawyer who lives in a lavish home in a little country village outside of Rochester, N.Y. once told us. "Next to my husband, the most important person I know is the young man who cleans our septic tank. Without him, country living would cease."

If you have properly researched your market, you know that there are enough clients who need your services. You also know that you and what you are doing is important. Because you *know* these things, you can be relaxed and confident when you solicit business. If you still develop "butterflies in the stomach" when you approach a prospect, try the listening technique. To do this effectively, you start with a question designed to elicit the prospect's observations about any given subject, preferably one you know he or she is interested in. You then find something in his comments with which you can agree. This starts the conversation rolling. You will find yourself relaxing and able to go into your sales pitch comfortably and effectively.

TAKING "FREE" IDEAS

Listening carefully is the easiest way to get ideas of people's needs.

When Sandy Schoene heard her bridge partners talking about their teenagers' search for "campy, kicky clothes — you know the things they wore in the twenties," she remembered the trunks of things she had brought to the Salvation Army Thrift Shop. On her way home from the bridge game, she stopped at the shop and bought the four fur coats in the store for $10.00. At home, she phoned one of the teenagers and invited her and her friends to see the coats. At $10 a piece the girls snatched them up as great finds and commissioned Sandy to find some more. That was the beginning of Sandy's Shop for Sumptuous Scavengers. She decorated her basement in art nouveau style, using thrift shop furniture and old movie star posters, and kept her inventory up by making the rounds of rummage sales, church fairs and auctions. Continuing to listen carefully, she was able to determine what items would be most in demand and what prices the traffic would bear. "I almost feel guilty," Sandy told us, "taking a 500% mark-up or more on some things, but I like adding up my bank deposits at the end of the week."

Ideas can be taken from books, magazines and trade journals. While you cannot infringe on anyone's patent, copyright or registered name, if you can develop profitable ideas for utilizing them you can often secure the rights for modest fees. The United States Patent Office, Washington, D.C. periodically publishes lists of patents which have been granted. Perusing these lists may give you ideas for new devices of your own or for applications of the newly patented items.

The successful enterpreneur is constantly seeking and using new ideas to assure business growth. The more novel the approach the more attention the business can secure.

USING CLIENTS TO GET MORE CLIENTS

Successful people have a way of using other people for their own advantage. That may sound crass, but it need not be. It can be as innocent as asking people to help you, and often both parties can derive substantial benefits.

You can ask your clients to recommend you to others by word of mouth. Or you can ask your clients to write you a letter with their favorable impressions of your product or service. If you secure permission from those who write these testimonials or endorsements, you can use them or parts of them in your advertising. You might also prepare a folder or scrapbook of such letters to show to prospective clients.

Research has indicated that what others say about you, your product or your service is more credible than what you yourself say in your ads. That's why the "testimonial approach" is often used in major advertising campaigns. Celebrities are often paid to give such testimonials because there is a tendency for their followings to be influenced by them. Others who give testimonials or endorsements which are to be used commercially receive discounts on the products or services.

A health club offers an extension of one month's membership in return for every new client a member signs up. A contest bulletin extends a subscription by four issues for each new subscriber recommended by a current subscriber.

These techniques can be applied to your business in many ways. If you cannot work out a discount or extension of service, you might consider an inexpensive but useful gift as a token of appreciation. Or you might develop a system whereby premiums are given when ten or more new clients are recommended.

The use of "case studies" or "case histories" is another technique which uses your current clients to attract new ones. The study or history is simply an article, generally written in feature form, of approximately 1,000 words telling how your product or service is utilized by an individual, organization or business. The article explains why your product or service was chosen, its benefits in the particular instance, and the advantages the user finds in it over previous or alternate products or services. The study is based on an interview with the individual responsible for choosing or using the product or service, and is usually accompanied by photos. When complete, these articles can be used as sales pieces, feature news releases, or trade journal stories. To be effective for these purposes, the studies should be done professionally. The average cost of approximately $500 plus any expenses incurred is reasonable when compared to advertising costs.

VENTURING INTO ALLIED FIELDS

You can benefit from the confidence of your clients by offering them additional products and services. Customers often clue you into unfulfilled needs. Printers discover clients need someone to create effective direct mail letters. Advertising agencies learn that public relations services are needed. Dressmakers often find that their customers need custom made draperies and spreads. Caterers are frequently asked about cleaning services. Sandy Schoene added foreign imports and handmade accessories to her thrift shop inventory because the mother of teenage daughters expressed a need for "something new and different."

Bert S. ventured into the allied field of floor coverings when he sensed a changing trend. Others go into the allied fields because existing business growth is not as rapid as anticipated and there is time and manpower available.

Filling such secondary needs can increase your profits from existing clientele and open new markets for your initial services. Returns on the new venture may outstrip those from the original business. Even if they do not, the overall profit picture can be improved if the additional service increases the utilization of equipment and manpower.

The profit potential of each new venture should be carefully analyzed using the yardsticks you learned in Chapter 1. While many new ventures will test out favorably, you need not write off the others completely. Many successful fortune builders have added to their capital by arranging for referral fees for projects they couldn't undertake themselves.

WINNING OVER COMPETITION EVERY TIME

Every summer, Patti worked as a waitress at an adult sports camp, she wound up with more tips than any of the others. Not only that, but returning guests always asked to be seated at Patti's section of the dining room. What did Patti do that enabled her to win out every time? She anticipated requests, remembered individual preferences, went out of her way to meet every special need graciously, and performed her duties efficiently and with a smile — even when her feet ached.

Like Patti, you can win out over competition every time if you provide a consistently good service or product individualized to meet the special needs of special clients. You can develop and keep a loyal clientele by keeping flexible hours and flexible responses to requests. You can personalize your customer relations by remembering to send hand-signed cards for birthdays, anniversaries or other happy events and suitable expressions of condolence when necessary. As more and more customer relations become computerized and impersonal, individualized attention, graciously given, pays handsome dividends. People appreciate having their complaints promptly answered and remedied. Customers stay with and recommend concerns which try harder to meet their needs.

Oddly enough, many business firms do not recognize these basic business concepts. If you accept them and implement them you will not find competition a problem.

X-RAYING YOUR ORGANIZATION FOR MAXIMUM PROFIT

Larry P, whose lawn and garden maintenance firm served several hundred development homes, saved thousands of man-hours by changing from hand-rakes to vacuum cleaners for grass clippings and autumn leaves. Since he received the same flat fee for each job, the savings were clear profit.

Just because something has always been done one way is insufficient justification to keep doing it that way. Each phase of the operation must be examined. The object is to always improve productivity and to reduce costs. Labor saving devices, such as Larry's vacuum cleaners, should be viewed on a cost to profit increase basis to see whether their investment is justified. •

The analysis should cover not only the production or service process but also so-called fixed expenses — rent, heat, power, and light, vehicles, telephone, postage, secretarial or bookkeeping help, etc. The use of brief handwritten carbon copy memos can reduce toll charges and provide confirmation records as well. Free lance or contract services might reduce secretarial and bookkeeping costs.

You know your business far better than any costly business analyst or consultant does. The fees you pay for such analysis can be saved if you use X-ray vision — a piercing insight without respect for the old ways and without prejudice for the new.

YESSING YOUR WAY TO BUSINESS OPPORTUNITIES

So many successful service businesses have grown out of the "Yes, We Can Do That" response to unusual requests that there ought to be a firm with the name. It makes sense. A request is an explanation of need. If you can fill the need at a profit, why not?

The "Yes" reply can not only increase business volume, it can change the entire character of the business. Bob F. became a wealthy auctioneer via an oil burner service business. One spring day as Bob supervised a burner check-up, the housewife asked if he knew anyone who could clean out the cellar. "My crew can do it," Bob replied. "Summer's a slow season for us." The cellar cleaning business expanded to include attics and garages — and to an accumulation of trash and treasures. That started the auction service. The housewives were delighted to pay for cartage to the auction barn and a 20% commission, and Bob hung out his shingle as "The Cleanest Colonel."

Yessing your way to business opportunities only requires confidence in yourself and your abilities to accomplish anything you really want to. That's worth remembering!

ZEROING IN ON YOUR SPECIAL FORTUNE

There are people who make a fortune in bad times and there are people whose fortunes rise from seemingly unlikely sources. Junkmen have become millionaires and garbage removal services are big and profitable business. Both men and women have cashed in on needlework. A college student became independently wealthy supplying goody packages to campus colleagues. An assortment of herb seeds started a successful food columnist on her way.

There are needs to fill everywhere. Your talents, no matter how you yourself underestimate them, are keys to hundreds of business opportunities. As you read this book, you may find yourself overwhelmed by ideas which can start you on your way to independence and security for the rest of your life.

But the crucial factor goes beyond the need, over and above the ideas. The vital ingredient for success is the ability to zero in on your target. "Sticktuition" is worth more than tuition to the best school in the world. Perserverance is probably one of the most valuable talents you can develop. Problems and difficulties which seem almost insurmountable when you think about them are often reduced to proportions you can handle when you begin to handle them. Students know that the hardest part of their studies is getting down to work.

You can develop the ability to zero in on a money making project. You simply take a leaf from the air force. You map out your program, make full speed to your target and give it all you've got.

3

HOW TO BUILD A BUSINESS
FILLING THE NEEDS
OF BUSINESS

HOW MRS. MILEY GOT THE KEYS TO THE BANK
JOANNE MILEY'S AFTER-HOURS SERVICE

When Craig Miley was seriously injured, his wife, Joanne simply had to support the family. But she also had to stay home with the invalid until the older children came home from school. One of our clients asked us if we could make any suggestions.

"I've never worked before," Joanne told us. "About the only things I know how to do really well are cook and clean, and Craig needs me home during the day."

"Why don't you call that new bank in the shopping center," we suggested. Joanne was incredulous. "I can't borrow money now — we're in hock up to our necks."

"Not to borrow money," we pointed out. "To start an after-hours business of your own. The bank has been having trouble keeping a janitor or so it would appear from the ads they keep running in the classified. They might need a dependable cleaning service."

The bank had been paying the janitor minimum wage for a 40 hour week. As an employee, the janitor was covered by social security, workmen's compensation and unemployment insurance. In addition, he was eligible for employee fringe benefits, paid vacations, health insurance, and a pension. Altogether, these "Extras" cost the bank more than 25% above the salary.

Mrs. Miley estimated that she could do the job in two hours a night, five nights a week. She offered to secure a bond and to contract for the bank cleaning work for a fee slightly less than the janitor's weekly salary.

The bank manager recognized it as an economical answer to his problem. Mrs. Miley had her first client. Three weeks later, after the area bankers' monthly luncheon, Mrs. Miley was contacted by two other banks. She knew she could handle one more. But, two? She hired a neighbor to work for her at hourly rates, and then another. To the daily cleaning routine, she's added — at extra fees, of course — window washing, rug and furniture shampooing, and drapery dry cleaning by arrangement with a local cleaner.

Banks are not the only businesses which need cleaning services. Professional offices of all kinds are good prospects. Contacting new building developers or renting agencies may provide many new customers.

With six employees and three panel trucks, attractively lettered "Joanne Miley's After-Hours Service" Joanne Miley now knows that, in addition to cooking and cleaning, she knows how to run a business filling the needs of business.

THE NEEDS OF BUSINESS YOU CAN FILL

Nearly every business or industry has certain needs which can be filled more economically or more beneficially by outsiders, i.e., contractors rather than by payroll employees. In most instances, those are needs which are not directly or immediately involved with the function of the business. In addition, those needs which do not really require full-time services of an employee can often be filled by outsiders.

For example, XYZ Company's main function is to manufacture and sell widgets. To perform its main function the company needs employees to work the widget-making machines, to wrap and package the widgets, and to sell them to distributors. Not immediately and directly involved with the production and sales function, but necessary to it in varying degrees are such functions as cleaning the plant, getting rid of trash and waste material, transporting products or people, and, possibly, providing access to soft drinks and snacks for its employees.

Many industries will pay far more than employee's salaries to outsiders who can fill special or particular needs. In general, these require one-time or periodic, rather than routine, service. Alternatively, they may be needs which require or would benefit from outside objectivity, specialization or expertise. For example, a firm might turn to an outside consultant if it required a management study or evaluation, or interior decorating for its new executive suite, or energy saving reviews of heat, light and power processes.

HOW YOU CAN ANALYZE ANY BUSINESS FOR NEEDS YOU CAN FILL

If you use the investigative techniques discussed earlier in this book you can find out the specific needs of most businesses and industries. You can also secure copies of the trade journals of the particular field. These newspapers and magazines discuss specific problems facing the industry. Reading these journals serves a twofold purpose. It serves as an idea germinator because where there are problems, there are needs; and it helps you accumulate a list of potential customers for your idea, product or service. To locate the trade journal(s) for any particular field, check the Standard Rate and Data publication available at many libraries and at all advertising agencies. This publication lists trade magazines and papers by subject.

A SIMPLE MENTAL EXERCISE

A simple mental exercise, however, can lubricate your thinking machine and stimulate your own jackpot of profitable ideas. The exercise can be done any place and anytime, if there are no distractions. You can do it alone or with one or several partners. All you need is a pencil and paper. What you do is *simply to visualize as much as you can of the entire business cycle of any operation.* As you do this, record the needs you see which fit into the categories we've discussed.

A BAKER'S DOZEN BUSINESS NEEDS

Here is just one list of needs of a small manufacturing company:

1. To improve a product
2. To manufacture a product less expensively
3. To test new products
4. To dispose of rejects, seconds, and overruns
5. To publicize, advertise, or otherwise promote business
6. To handle complaints and criticism
7. To collect past due bills
8. To create a new trademark
9. To deliver products
10. To develop a pension plan for employees
11. To reduce or eliminate theft
12. To expand or diversify
13. To secure additional capital.

THE DIRECTORY OF DISCOUNT SHOPS AND OUTLETS

There are many people who have started successful businesses of their own by filling need #4 — the need of factories to dispose of products which cannot be sold to prime buyers. If your area has consumer goods factories and they do not have their own outlet shops, you might contact them with various proposals. You could offer to run an outlet shop for their merchandise exclusively or for the merchandise of several manufacturers. You could offer to purchase quantities of merchandise at low enough prices to resell it to exporters or to retail discount shops. Or you might undertake on a commission basis to find buyers for the products.

Although John and Elizabeth W. held reasonably good jobs, they yearned to own and run a business of their own. Spare time was used to check out businesses they heard or read about. On a company sponsored convention held in a New England city, they heard about a shop that sold "silver seconds" at low, low prices. They visited the store along with masses of other conventioners who had obviously heard about the shop too. It appeared that everyone needed or felt they couldn't pass up the bargain silverware, trays, teapots, etc.

As John and Elizabeth's home was close to a convention type city, they began thinking about a "silver lining" business for themselves. It took some time before they were able to locate and negotiate with three well-known china manufacturers who had a continuing supply of "seconds" and were interested in disposing of them. The dishes ran from individual pieces to full sets...all seconds and all at super-discount prices when purchased in bulk. The couple began a search for a low rent store in their suburb. Even before they signed a lease, they began researching convention magazines, checking with convention managers of the city hotels, and looking through area newspapers for news of conventions scheduled for their city. Wherever possible, they obtained names and addresses of the leadership of the conventions for direct mailing pieces about their new shop. The couple also scheduled an advertising campaign directed to visitors to the city and to all convention groups arriving.

Elizabeth does the firm's books and indicated that their initial china purchases amounted to $6,000. They listed their store in all city "what to do" columns, and publications devoted to conventioners. Their first year investment in the store rental and renovation amounted to another $4,500. Their annual advertising budget amounted to $2,200. Return visits and word of mouth advertising from happy customers augmented this. First year sales, according to the couple hit $45,000, and the figures have been going up ever since. Mark-up is running about 110% over cost and in some instances, where the buy is especially good, even more. Expenses are kept to a minimum, except in the area of advertising which is an on-going and often a rising cost. The store is not fancy and requires only shelves and a number of tables set up to display the china in table setting patterns. The china "seconds" are not perishable (except for a few daily customer drops) and people come back year after year to replenish or build their own sets.

John and Elizabeth have built a sound business of their own using OPN and they didn't have to travel to China to accomplish it.

But, even if all of the area manufacturers have their own or established outlets for their products, all is not lost. You can turn a neat profit filling the need to let people know where these outlets are, what they sell, their shopping hours and days, and their payment policies. Your *City or Regional Directory of Discount Shops and Outlets* can be inexpensively reproduced by photo-offset printing. You could sell it by mail using classified ads in regional papers. The directories might also be sold by area motels, hotels and tourist attractions, as well as at neighborhood newsstands and bookshops.

So you see, there are many ways that business needs can fill your till. It just depends on what specific interests and talents you want to use. We read recently of two young Ivy League college graduates who gave up promising careers in a large law firm to open their own industrial trash collecting business in a suburban area where municipal garbage removal was not a practice.

DISCOVERING YOUR OWN BUSINESS SPECIALTY MARKET

In Chapter 2 we discussed how you can assess your own assets and abilities and classify your scope of interests. Do you have artistic talents and are you interested in using them commercially? Then, you would look to firms which require sign painting, posters, packaging designs, layout work, trademarks or logos, etc. You might find these as industrial firms or businesses or as advertising agencies which serve them. In the former case, you might wind up with an art agency of your own as your clientele grows. In the latter case, if you serve enough agencies, you could wind up as a specialist.

JIM H'S TARGET TECHNIQUE FOR BULL'S EYE DOLLARS

The old adage about "one picture being worth a thousand words" is especially true when you're attempting to promote your new commercial art business.

Jim H., who lived in a Midwest city that was heavy with industries, used a "target technique" to obtain his clients. He first chose a half-dozen firms that he felt looked like good prospects. Next, he obtained newspaper and trade papers carrying ads by the firms he had selected. He then developed a concept of his own about each of the firms and developed an artwork piece to complement the concept. Next, he determined exactly who was responsible for the advertising in each of the six firms and directed his "art-ad-concept" to the responsible individual for review. Each concept was accompanied by a simple letter that explained his service and his effort to earn their business. Two of the six firms contacted liked his original approach and retained his services. Three firms never bothered to answer and one firm responded negatively.

Jim continued his "target technique" until he built a clientele for his commercial art talents. Now, whenever things get slow or when he feels that new clients should be added to his roster of customers, he resorts to the same program.

The same "target technique" can be used to zero in OPN opportunities for any of your skills in the business world.

Do your skills lie in writing and your interests in people? Then you might investigate the need for publicity releases or public information programs. Or you might consider writing the copy for advertising brochures or newspaper advertising. Or, you might discover, in your research, that each year thousands of businesses celebrate an important milestone and might become clients for anniversary or commemorative booklets.

Or would you rather be on wheels? How many department stores in your area have their own delivery vehicles? If you combined the deliveries of several stores, correctly routed, and efficiently coordinated couldn't you deliver the goods at a savings to the store and a profit to yourself? United Parcel Service (UPS) grew out of the need for less costly, more rapid dependable delivery that went beyond the services of Railway Express and the

United States Postal Service. And, with increasing costs of/U.S. postage, many firms are turning to private contractors particularly for in-city deliveries of mail messages, valuable papers, etc.

One by one, write down each of your skills, talents, and interests. Next to each, make a list of all the tasks these assets and abilities enable you to do. Then take your analysis of business needs and match them up. Chances are that you'll discover more than one specialty business you can get into easily.

HOW TO SOLICIT BUSINESS FROM
BUSINESS AND INDUSTRY

Having determined that there is a need you can profitably fill, the object is to get the opportunity to do just that.

If the existing need is strong and there is no competition to fill it, the mailing of a simple announcement of your new business or service will suffice to bring you inquiries from potential clients.

If you have friends or relatives who have contacts among businessmen who could use your idea, service, or product, they should be well informed about your plans. When you are providing a legitimate answer to a legitimate need, you're really doing something worthwhile. Your friends and relatives could very well be doing their business contacts a favor by telling them about you.

If your potential clients are many or distant, you can solicit business by direct mail. Mailing lists can be purchased from list companies, or you may develop your own using telephone books, city directories, and the trade journals we discussed previously.

If your service is directed chiefly to a single region, a series of small advertisements in the area paper will develop leads for you. If your endeavor will deal specifically with one type of business or industry, you should consider advertising in the applicable trade journal or paper.

If you have the time and can make yourself feel comfortable doing it, the best way to sell yourself is in person. Call or write for an appointment with your potential client. When you get that meeting, talk directly, explaining what you can do and how the client's business will benefit. From your analysis of business needs you will be able to speak knowledgeably, increasing confidence in your ability to carry through.

If you're not disturbed by an occasional rebuff, you don't have to wait for an appointment. Simply stop in and ask to see the decisionmaker to discuss your proposal. If the proper individual is not available, you can leave your card, requesting a phone call or a future appointment.

The most important thing to remember is that you are honestly presenting a genuine solution to one of their real problems. You are going to help them fill a need. The only thing they will have to do is pay you. Keeping this in mind will make it easy to approach anyone, no matter how large or prestigious his business.

SUMMARY-CHECKLIST FOR SOLICITING BUSINESS

_____Announcement Cards

_____Friends, Relatives, Associates list

_____Small ads in area newspapers

_____Ads in applicable trade journals

_____Direct mail to appropriate lists

_____Personal solicitation

FINDING YOUR PROFITS IN SHOPPING CENTERS

The merchants who operate businesses in shopping centers pay high rentals to share the potential benefits of high customer traffic. You don't have to spend a pretty penny to take your cut of the profits. In fact, you can earn a considerable income catering to the needs of shopping centers. All it really takes is an understanding of how these centers operate.

The shopping center or mall is a cluster of retail stores located on one land parcel or strip, or under one roof. In most instances a developer or owner builds these centers and leases space to as wide a variety of stores as possible. In the process, three distinct entities are created. These are: the owner or developer who is represented at the center by a mall manager; the individual merchant who may be a large department store manager, a chain store manager, or the owner of the store; and the merchants association which is an organization composed of all of the merchants in the center. In usual practice, the owner is also a member of the merchants association and contributes dues representing between 1/4 and 1/3 of the merchants' dues assessments.

Each of these entities have special needs which can effectively be filled by outsiders. But the prime need of a shopping center is customer traffic, for without it there is no business. To promote such traffic, individual stores use advertising and promotional efforts of their own. In addition, the association of merchants as a group seek traffic building attractions and promotions. If you consider that there are 52 weeks in every year and that every shopping center needs attractions and promotions, you'll recognize how great an opportunity there is for you.

WHOM TO SEE FOR WHAT IN A SHOPPING CENTER

Mall or Center Manager (Reports To Developer)	All service contracts for center proper; i.e.-Security, traffic control, cleaning maintenance, snow removal, communications systems, etc.
Store Owners or Managers	All services required by an individual store: i.e.-Advertising, signs, banners, displays, sales promotion with store, exhibits, contests, fashion shows, etc., product repairs, alterations, etc.
Merchants Association Executive	All promotional efforts for entire center: i.e.-shows, exhibits, displays, traffic builders, advertising, public relations, etc.

Using the imaginating technique, we can visualize many of these needs and develop some ideas on how to fill them. Our list might look something like this:

TRAFFIC BUILDING NEEDS OF SHOPPING CENTERS

Need	*Skill Required To Fill*
Signs, banners & posters	lettering, art, design (or ability to hire skill)
Newspaper advertising design	lettering, art, design (or ability to hire skill)
Handbills and flyers	lettering, art, design (or ability to hire skill), printing
Radio commercial	copywriting, dramatic voice presentation, taping copy
Television commercial	script-writing, filming, dramatic talent
Promotional ideas	observation, research, imagination, follow-through
Special attractions	any demonstrable skill, ability to organize crowd-drawing activities, ability to capitalize on hobby, special interest, or talent; arts and crafts; etc.
Community relations	ability to deal with people; knowledge of community organization functions or ability to research them.
Special services	skills depend on services which might include shopping center baby-sitting service or day nursery; personal shopper service; center delivery service; personalizing-monogramming service; etc.

There can be endless subdivisions of each of these areas. Seasonal attractions, for example, create the need for costumes to rent or purchase. Creative home-sewers could successfully contract for costumes to dress Father Time; Santa Claus (and his helping elves); Cupid; the Easter Bunny; Uncle Sam; Farmer Jones; The Pilgrims; Thanksgiving Turkey; Storyland figures, etc. Costume rental agencies currently fill only a portion of this need (and might be investigated as another outlet for your products), but the demand can be promoted to far outstrip the existing supply.

Another talent frequently needed by individual stores as well as by merchants associations is that of the fashion show narrator and/or coordinator. While this is commonly thought to be a ladies' field, male narrators and coordinators may develop prestigious followings and their services are in demand.

HOW SALLY B. FASHIONED AN OPN CAREER

Mrs. Sally B. enjoyed buying and wearing nice clothing ever since she was a freshman in high school. Unfortunately, the cost of rearing a family put a slight damper on her personal clothing expenditures. The dollar crunch didn't dampen her enthusiasm for the finer things, however, and she managed to keep up with the latest in fashions by visiting clothing shops and reading the fashion magazines and newspapers.

One day in one of the better shops in her home town in Westchester, N.Y. she happened to overhear the owner telling the manager of the store about a proposed fashion show scheduled for the shopping center mall. Everything had been arranged from the models and clothing to the stage. The narrator (or person who described the clothing as the models came out on stage) had suddenly developed laryingitis and was unable to participate. Acting on impulse, Sally offered to do the narration and convinced the owner of her fashion expertise.

It was a simple task for Sally and the show went off beautifully. Her background in clothing stood her in good stead and her ready knowledge of current fashions permitted her to easily discuss the clothes as they were modeled. The owner of the shop rewarded her with an expensive dress and for the moment Sally was satisfied.

After the show, she discussed the day's activities with her husband. Why not, they conjectured, make a business out of fashion shows? And, this is just what Sally B. did. She began by attending a number of outstanding fashion shows put on by professionals. She watched, listened and took notes. Out of the information she acquired, Sally developed a program that she felt would go well in the many shopping centers surrounding her home. She then began to solicit personally and by mail the managers of the better dress shops and the promotional managers of the malls detailing her services. In a short time, she was called on to put on a fashion show in conjunction with a "Back To School" promotion co-sponsored by the mall promotion people and a number of shops catering to the teenage set. Other calls followed and Sally B. had a business of her own.

In order to remain completely flexible, Sally divided her fashion show services into a number of optional sections offering to provide part or all of the program. For example, for $100 a show, she will gather the information about the clothes to be modeled from the supplying store and write and present the narration. If the same show is to be presented more than once in one day, she charges $75 for the first repeat and $50 per show thereafter.

If Sally has to put on the complete show, starting from scratch, supplying the models and backstage help, the fee runs from $500 to $1000 depending on the number of models she must hire (which in turn depends on the number of fashion changes to be presented in the scheduled time) and the extent of elaborate settings, background, music, lighting, etc.

Last year, Sally B. brought $9,500 home to the family kitty, working part-time at something she enjoyed.

There is also always a need for seamstress and tailoring talents for alterations. While some of the more exclusive shops can afford to keep these people on their staffs, the vast majority of ready-to-wear retailers will be happy to refer their alterations to you if you are competent, accessible and obliging. The need in most areas is generally so great that you may need to recruit associates or employees on a full or part-time basis in order to meet your commitments.

Any skill or talent which you can demonstrate before small or large audiences can help you fill the needs of the shopping center circuit. Can you put on a whimsical puppet show? Is ventriloquism part of your parlour games? Magic shows, animal tricks, cartooning or caricaturing, are among the programs that have enabled people to book themselves into shopping centers throughout the country, fitting the geography into their travel plans or climate preferences.

Showmanship isn't limited to the performing arts we generally think of. Many stores and centers seek out cooking demonstrations, particularly those with an ethnic flavor or those which employ new kitchen equipment. The recent growing interest in arts and crafts of all types has prompted a search for talents to demonstrate these skills. Macrame makers, weavers, needleworkers, woodcarvers, jewelry-makers, glassblowers, leather crafters, etc., who make a presentable appearance and create a showmanship atmosphere can also establish a profitable schedule of demonstrations and store-sponsored classes.

Many talented people do not have the ability to sell themselves or to administer the profit-making details of their schedules. If by nature, you are an organizer or an administrator, you can develop a great business filling the mutual needs of these talented people and the shopping center or merchants association. By keeping a roster of available artists or craftsmen, or special interest people in any field (stamp or coin traders, or antique dealers, or camping equippers, for example) you can book an entire show into a center without any cost to the center itself. You make your money by charging each talent or trader either a fixed fee or a percentage of his sales. A successful show, i.e., one that builds traffic and elicits favorable press and customer response, is generally booked from year to year. Some centers will re-run a successful show seasonally. Many artists and craftsmen make the bulk of their income from these shows and will travel large distances to participate in them. It is quite possible to organize these traffic builders for centers in a three-hundred mile radius of your home, using word-of-month or newspaper solicitation for talent.

Though Richard G. dabbled a bit in oils, he couldn't really call himself an artist. His business oriented mind, however, discovered a void he believed he could fill for a great many artistic people.

After attending innumerable local art shows at schools, churches and parks, Richard concluded that the majority of artists had very little, if any, business talent. They hunted out shows to display their wares on a hit and miss basis. Sometimes, when lucky, they set up at a good show and sold a couple of pieces. More often than not, they spent the day in the sun with little to show for it besides a sunburn.

Enclosed shopping malls, decided Richard, were a natural showcase for art. They are weather-proof, year-round, and by the nature of the business constantly need to draw people of all ages, economic backgrounds, and interests.

Richard put his art business plan into operation. He began by collecting the business cards or names and addresses of every artist and craftsman he could locate. He attended art shows over a large area to build his initial list of several hundred potential exhibitors. Next, he prepared a letter to the promotional managers of malls throughout the region he wished to service, offering to put on professional art shows at no cost to the shopping center. The only requests he made to the promotion manager was that the show be scheduled at least 6 weeks time prior to the target date and that he be supplied with a floor plan of the space to be used in the mall. He also asked for the normal advertising support of the mall to promote the art show prior to and during the event.

The letters to the promotional managers drew an immediate response. The first show was scheduled just prior to the Christmas holiday season.

Richard sent out a mailing announcing the show to his artists' mailing list. Each artist, the letter indicated, would be assigned a selected spot inside one of the largest malls in the area. The season was just right for buying art and the crowds would be flocking to the shopping center 12 hours a day. In return for this opportunity, Richard indicated that there would be a service charge of only $20 per space.

By return mail, Richard received thirty responses. By the time show day rolled around, ten more artists had joined the show. Each artist was responsible for bringing his own display equipment, tables, chairs, etc. Richard was responsible for all relationships with mall management, for assigning the space locations to the exhibitors and for general supervision. The show was a great success for both Richard and the artists who had real opportunities to show and sell their creative works.

Richard grossed $800 on the first show, a two day event, and netted about $500. He had invested in a small amount of supplementary advertising to promote the show in two local newspapers.

From that point on, Richard had a "show business" of his own built on OPN. Incidentally, a few months after he got started in his new business, he decided to take advantage of the shows himself. He made arrangements with two homebound artists to display and sell their art at each show for a commission. Figuring that he had to oversee the programs anyway, he was able to add extra dollars to his income.

A word of caution is in order here. While the vast majority of artists and craftsmen are truly beautiful people, some are highly tempermental, erratic and not wholly dependable. Show managers have to develop high standards and firm rules to fill the requirements of each particular center. By and large, the "storekeepers" who form the merchants association are managers working for chains. These men and women are typically conservative in attitude and do not generally favor "far-out" types.

What may be acceptable to one culture may be offensive to another. When one does business with a shopping center, he or she will be dealing with 50 to 100 individual merchants. They, in turn, are doing business with thousands of customers of varying backgrounds and tastes.

The simple solution, to the seemingly insurmountable problem, is to lay out ground rules at the very beginning of the association. The artist who will be displaying in the shopping center must understand that there is a difference between sloppy and dirty clothing and attractive way-out attire. They must realize that there may be many culture differences and that, for example, nursing an infant in open view is not generally acceptable. They must understand that "hawking" or pulling people into their booth area is taboo and that honesty in product sales is a must because any ill-will generated is against the shopping center as well as the artist.

Shopping centers also require a whole gamut of services in addition to traffic building. You can develop a business contracting for snow removal, interior and exterior cleaning, window cleaning, landscaping, communications systems and traffic and security control, to name just a few services which are frequently contracted from outsiders.

While newly developing centers would seem to provide your best market for such service contracts, established centers offer a great potential. We have rarely come across a center whose management is completely satisfied with existing services on staff arrangements. Mall managers, whose well paid jobs depend on the efficient operation of all aspects of the center are generally receptive to proposals for better meeting their needs.

PROTECTING YOUR INTERESTS

Special licenses are usually not required to contract services to a shopping center, except, possibly, in the areas of food services which come under health codes. Liability insurance for programs and promotions is usually carried by all shopping centers. If the program has any special hazards, you may also be asked to supply liability insurance coverage to additionally protect the merchant's association and the landlord of the shopping center. In this case, you can purchase a special short-term policy from your local agent to cover the particular program. This coverage might be essential for a program or display that involved animals. Persons attending a pet show might conceivably be bitten, or in some way or other bothered by an animal and they might seek financial redress. Your insurance will protect you from these claims.

Service contractors should check with an attorney and an accountant to make sure they file the necessary legal papers required by their state, city and county. These might include a DBA (Doing Business As) certificate, sales tax registration, etc. Requirements for state and federal unemployment insurance, disability insurance, workmen's compensation insurance, etc. should also be checked if you have any employees. If you are going to provide any equipment you should carry a comprehensive fire and theft policy as well as liability insurance.

A LITERAL FORTUNE IF YOU CAN FILL THIS NEED

The individual who solves the most serious current need of merchants will quickly generate a fortune. The fastest way to this fortune is to develop some device or product, approach or procedure which will reduce losses from employee theft and shoplifting. By studying the devices currently in the field, you may very well develop an improved version or a completely new approach to the problem. It's worth thinking about!

FILLING THE SPECIAL NEEDS OF
RESORTS, HOTELS AND MOTELS

In the lobby of one of the major Catskill hotels a crowd gathers after dinner to watch an artist deftly draw a caricature of a pair of newlyweds. That quick sketch completed, the couple is supplanted by a youngster shepherded by an obviously doting grandfather.

We have never seen that quick draw artist when there was not a long line of paying subjects waiting to be exaggerated on canvass.

At this resort and in resorts throughout the nation there is a prime need to provide as varied a format of guest entertainment and activities as possible. Particularly when resort hotels cater to conventions, a variety of offerings becomes part of the highly competitive sales picture. Because the resort business is so highly competitive, not only within regional areas but also in the framework of nationally and internationally known facilities and cruises, there is a tremendous need for singular and diverse attractions which will not cost hotel management much if any money. This need makes it possible for those with special talents or social skills to turn them into money making opportunities.

HOW MORRIS P. PAINTED MONEY

Morris P. is an instant-artist, who can fill a modest size canvas in ten minutes with an attractive scene of people, the sea or a landscape.

One summer, he was vacationing at a resort that also catered to convention groups. As he walked along the convention booths, he had a sudden urge to paint a scene that captured his imagination. A booth in the middle of the hall was empty because an exhibitor had not shown up. Morris asked permission to set up his canvas and easel in the booth and to paint. The request was granted.

Morris' painting speed and work drew an instant audience. People surrounded him and asked questions about his ability to produce work so rapidly and Morris responded jokingly with answers. Other members of the audience asked Morris to paint a specific picture for them offering to pay for his work. At that moment, Morris P. knew he had a new business.

He checked with the convention office of the hotel to find out what good sized conventions were due in the near future and the name of the convention group official to contact for a booth. When the convention opened, Morris set up his canvas and easel in the booth and rapidly began to paint. Just as before, he drew an audience, only this time, he was prepared with a patter of jokes and conversation and a price for his instant-art. He had come prepared with standard sized canvases and frames. He set prices on his work: $25 for a small framed original requested by one of the conventioners; $40 for a large size. By the time the three-day convention had concluded, Morris had taken in $1600 and had special orders for five additional paintings.

Morris P. now subscribes to the major convention journals and attends as many of the good sized conventions as his time schedule will permit. His speed, gift-of-gab and art talent is becoming a by-word on the convention circuit and is now being sought out by convention leadership to liven up the display areas. He's even had to put on shows for the wives of convention groups. Not only was he paid for the shows but he also sold the work he produced during the programs.

There are thousands of conventions held throughout the country each year. You can locate many of them through meetings and conventions magazines. If you have a talent as a quick-draw artist, caricaturist or cartoonist, you can do as well as Morris P.

The approach to hotel management (or to the program director, social director or convention manager) may be made by phone, mail or in person, depending on your accessibility to the resort. Each proposal should concisely explain what is being offered, the fee involved if the hotel were to pay for it directly, or the percentage which will be paid to the hotel if you are permitted to charge the guests directly.

Among the people we know who have turned their hobbies, interests and avocations into full time money makers are two folk dancing couples; a professional high school mathematics teacher who, with his wife, teach group classes in ballroom dancing, in return for the right to charge for private lessons; a widow who has turned her love of floral arrangements into a lucrative lecture demonstration service for women's convention groups; a cosmetician who puts on make-up demonstrations free and then sells the various lotions and potions which he uses to make people beautiful and a former barber who offers a men's hair styling program as a lead to hair piece sales.

A newspaper editor we know has capitalized on his family's interest and talent for bridge playing by providing bridge seminars and tournaments for several area hotels. On alternate evenings he runs bridge tournament opportunities for community players, at a charge of $1 per person.

Many resorts are anxious to lease various concessions to independent contractors. These range from bicycle rentals, which provide a steady but limited income, to sports pro shops for tennis, golf and skiing, which can provide extensive incomes.

The talent for telling a good story, for enjoying the companionship of people, for delivering special knowledge in any field, can help you fill the needs of resorts. Some of the best lecturers we know have developed a basic presentation running from fifteen minutes to an hour on a particular subject. By varying their introduction, their presentation has been made applicable to hundreds of convention groups. Incidentally the fee runs anywhere from $25 to several thousands depending on the degree of specialty and the prominence of the guest speaker.

A FLAIR FOR FASHION TALK

Convention programmers indicate that one of the most popular events for women's groups is the fashion show. If you have a flair for fashion talk or are willing to learn it, the need for fashion show coordinators and narrators can help you establish a lucrative and fascinating business.

To get started it is necessary to make contact with one or several prestige fashion shops. In return for generous mention of their names, these shops will provide, on a loan basis, the fashions to be shown, and a written description of each fashion and accessory. In some instances they will also provide a list of names of some of their regular customers who wear clothes well and who enjoy participating in fashion shows. Many of these can be cultivated to become unpaid models for your shows. Often, they are allowed to purchase the clothes they model at a discount.

In most cases, however, the models will come from the group

for whose benefit the show is scheduled. These volunteers should be perfect sizes so that they can wear the clothes without alteration. Depending on the length of the show, which usually does not run more than one hour, five to fifteen models are sufficient. The fewer the models the faster the changes of costume have to be made backstage.

The fashion show script is usually written around a special theme utilizing the seasons on various sports or activities. Depending on the budget, the backdrop can be very elaborate, or it can simply be a stage or runway. If background music is necessary, recordings or tapes can be used.

Fashion show coordinators and narrators are needed not only by resorts, hotels and motels. Department stores, specialty shops, and shopping centers periodically need such services. Small radio and television stations occasionally employ such programs to increase advertising. Fashionable restaurants might be persuaded to run a fashion show luncheon weekly as a traffic builder.

A profitable off-shoot of this business is the fashion column for local newspapers, penny-savers, and other area publications. Advertising managers of such publications are always alert to ways to expand their advertising income. The fashion-line column becomes a vehicle for advertising sales and provides a reader service at the same time. And, your by-line or the column really establishes you as a fashion expert, enhancing your fees as show coordinator.

GENERATING GROUP BUSINESS

Just as the main need of shopping centers is consumer traffic, the principal need of resorts, hotels and motels is paying guests. Every operating facility has a basic overhead — for taxes or rent, maintenance, essential staff and essential services. These costs exist whether the hotel has ten guests or a hundred. Other costs such as food, and service personnel wages, entertainment, etc. are prorated on a per person basis. These per person costs go up minimally, if at all, and are often reduced as the rate of occupancy goes up. It is for this reason that most hotels offer special inducements or rates for conventions or other group business.

Group sales become the function of the Convention Sales Office, or the Sales Manager. The men and women who serve in these capacities generally have two things going for them in addition to their administrative abilities. They have an extensive knowledge of existing groups and organization and their leadership; and they are good socializers or sales people.

No matter how competent these people are, they cannot be omnipresent nor omniscient. As a result there is frequently a need beyond the capacity of the sales office to generate business. Some of this is done by offering travel agents a percentage on group business they bring in. (The commission rate on group business is generally half the rate on individual full price business.) In recent years group business commissions have averaged 5%.

You do not have to be a travel agent to cash in on group sales. In some instances you do not even have to do the selling yourself. A number of hotels will pay you the applicable commission for generating the lead and arranging for the hotel staff to follow-up and clinch the sale.

These commissions can add up to a considerable income. Groups run from 24 to over a thousand. A typical group of 100 people — that's only 50 couples — for 3 days and 2 nights at a rate of $30 per person per day generates $6,000 in business for the hotel. At 5%, your commission would be $300. Often your own room and board is thrown in free if you want to join the group.

Every group you belong to is a potential for a convention, outing, conference, or low cost group vacation. If you are not a joiner yourself, you can nevertheless find out about the size, leadership and possibilities of area organizations (church and synagogues, service and civic clubs, bowling and athletic leagues, business associations, unions, social and fraternal groups, student "Class Day" groups and senior citizens' clubs, just to mention a few). You can then solicit these groups personally or by mail until you build up a following.

In recent years a number of successful group business ventures have centered on the so called "singles" groups. The singles market consists of single men and women from 18 to 80, widows, widowers, divorced and unmarried. The promoters of "singles" group business use varied approaches.

Some book a block of rooms themselves at a special reduced

rate and then by direct mail specifically to their carefully nur-tured lists of "singles" sell a full rate "package vacation." Others advertise in the singles sections of newspapers and magazines or at singles apartment complexes or clubs and make up a group from the total responses.

If you are interested in promoting group business of any type, you should become familiar with the properties you will be "sell-ing" and with the management at these hotels, motels, resorts, and even cruise lines. As long as you make it clear that you are a legit-imate operator and not a "free-loader," i.e., someone using a pre-text to have a free meal or lodging at the facility, most hotelmen will be happy to talk to you. The business arrangements, rates of commission, etc., discussed and negotiated at this time should be confirmed in writing. In addition to discussing first-year com-missions on groups you bring in, the following years' rates should also be agreed upon for your protection in the event that the group later books direct.

When you have developed a following of groups you may want to affiliate with an established travel agency or form your own to take advantage of transportation commissions as well, and to ex-pand your potential.

CREATING GROUPS

The singles promoter pioneered the approach to creating mut-ual interest vacationing groups. A vacation or seminar group can be created in similar fashion from almost any special interest market. On a cruise in January 1974 we met approximately 150 star gazers who had been booked as a group by a young man who promoted a "Kohoutec Package." Kohoutec, for those of you who aren't star-gazers, was a recently discovered comet that was sup-posed to put in an awesome appearance at the beginning of 1974. Unfortunately, for the astronomy lover, the comet was either poorly discernable or blocked by stars or clouds, so that very few without very powerful telescopes every actually viewed the sight. A ship at sea was supposed to be an ideal spot to view the comet and thus the promotion.

You can, if you start well enough in advance (at least six months), promote bridge seminar weekends or mid-weeks; nature study groups, fall foliage vacations, photography groups, antiquers' holidays; metropolitan shopping jaunts, etc.

The chief criteria to be used in attempting to create a group are: the size of interested potential market; the ease of reaching that market directly through trade or special interest magazines or journals; or the availability of lists for direct mail. These criteria determine the cost of developing a group. In addition, familiarity with the trade or special interest magazines provide calendars of previously scheduled events if any exist, so that major conflicts can be avoided. These publications are also generally receptive to publicity releases, particularly if some advertising is placed with them.

Barry G.'s travel organization or agency was grossing close to $200,000 in commissions a year when we met him. He began on a much smaller scale, of course, but every group trip that he took brought him commissions not only on the transportation, food and lodgings, but also on all purchases made at the specialty spots that he took the group to.

The individual who establishes himself or herself as a Convention Consultant or a Group Vacation Counselor can become a world traveler as well. One of the best traveled men we've ever met was a Texas gentleman whose twang was as sharp as a plucked rubber band. He had flown up to the Catskills in his own private plane to inspect a resort we represented. Among his luggage were several cases of imported beer.

"You really didn't have to bring your own," we chided.

"Well, you never know," he retorted. "I take a group of American brewers on a tour of European breweries every year, and I've become partial to this special brand."

HOW EDGEWOOD BECAME A PHOTOGRAPHER'S HOLIDAY

A few years ago, friends of ours became owners of a picturesque summer resort which had catered to a distinguished clientele for over half a century. With its elegant clientele becoming older, the Edgewood Inn, in Livingston Manor, N.Y., might have been destined for a historic place alongside several hundred other Catskill hotels which simply faded into the colorful countryside.

Instead, the hotel is currently adding rooms. Part of the reason, certainly, is the cordial and accomodating family management. But a contributing factor, we believe, is the emphasis placed on special interest groups. The first of these groups were photographers invited to a photographic seminar and shooting weekend. Working in cooperation with representatives of the leading trade journals and specialty magazines, a publicity campaign and a limited market advertising program was undertaken. A direct mail campaign was used to cover the various photography clubs within driving range.

The weekend was a sell-out and has become an annual event.

You can vacation free or afford to pay your own way when you fill the needs of hotels, motels, and exciting resorts. People will hardly believe that you're working.

4

HOW TO GET RICHER FILLING
THE NEEDS OF THE RICH

FINDING WEALTHY NEEDS

There are as many types of wealthy people as there are poor or middle-income categories. Each rich man or woman may have special needs which present fortune building opportunities. It's certainly possible to grow wealthy by filling the special needs of a special individual, but it is usually a slower route than catering to more universal needs in this moneyed market.

You can discover the needs of the rich by using the techniques discussed in Chapters 1 and 2. Put these techniques into a golden, glowing perspective by thinking the separate letters of the word RICH. R-I-C-H. RESEARCH-IMAGINATE-CONTACT-HONE IN.

R is for research. Autobiographies and biographies give valuable insights in the lifestyle of the wealthy. The society pages of newspapers and periodicals such as *Vogue* and *Harpers Bazaar, Fortune,* etc., all provide clues to the needs of the affluent. The advertisements designed to reach the well-heeled reader are worth looking into because they represent the costly research of others who have investigated the market. In addition, catalogues from department and specialty shops patronized by the wealthy can stimulate your thinking. Sometimes, too, these stores or their catalogue mailing agencies sell their lists of purchasers through mailing list firms. These list firms often can provide you with lists of people who fall into high income categories or who have special interests as indicated by subscriptions to special interest publications such as antiques, big game hunting, the arts, yachting, horse-breeding, etc.

I is for imaginate. As you do your research, picture yourself in the place of the millionaires and billionaires you are reading about. What are their specific needs? What are their dreams and aspirations? How can their lives be made easier, more pleasant, more exciting, more secure?

C is for contact. You can observe the habits of the wealthy by habituating the places they are apt to be. This gambit takes something of an investment, though not necessarily a great deal, but it can pay off handsomely. It doesn't cost much, if anything, to visit the Rolls Royce Showroom or the Ferarri's, the chic and expensive art and antique galleries, or the elegant, exclusive shops and boutiques which cater to the people in whom you're interested.

David B., who sells expensive sail boats and earns $30,000 or more each year, habituates the resort areas where the rich vacation. One of nine children from a poor farm family, David used to augment the family income by doing odd jobs around a marina after school. He liked the way the wealthy dressed and lived and spent their money. David vowed that one day he, too, would live like that and now he does. He makes his contacts by offering a $25 "commission" to hotel waiters, reservation clerks, marina hands and anyone else who gives him a lead to a sale. In addition, David spends about $200 a week dining in exclusive restaurants, working out in the gym, and entertaining prospects. "Give me ten contacts and I'll sell at least three," David says.

You can take a leaf from David's book. You can make it a practice to hang out where the rich live, work or play. You can make contact with the high and mighty on your own. You can also develop your contacts through their chauffeurs, secretaries, companions, doormen, service personnel, hairdressers, barbers and doctors. As David notes, "The closer you get to the rich, the more needs you discover you can fill."

H is for "hone in." The needs of the rich offer many exciting opportunities. As you examine them you may be tempted to go beyond imaginating into day-dreaming or fantasy. It is important to sharpen your focus on or *hone in on* the needs which match your own particular talents and interests. People have made a fortune, for example, filling the needs of modern art collectors, but if art is not your forte it's wise to seek another area for your business genius. On the other hand, if you have a special interest or skill in any field, you might earn more, faster if you cater to those who can afford to pay well for what they want.

Rollie J. learned to use a camera when he was recovering from polio. Still handicapped by a limp, Rollie nets over $20,000 a year snapping his shutter at conventions. He pays hotel convention managers 15% of his gross sales for recommending him to convention groups. An average convention is good for several hundred dollars worth of immediate sales. Rollie adds to that by selling newsworthy photos to wire services, newspapers and trade journals. "They only pay a few dollars per picture," Rollie notes, "but it adds up. More important, published pictures add to my prestige with convention groups, and lead to big money portrait sales."

TEN APPARENT NEEDS OF THE WEALTHY

Our own association with the rich and super-rich produced this list of needs:

1. The need for recognition
2. The need to set the pace
3. The need to be different
4. The need for humanitarian service
5. The need for money management
6. The need for personal and family safety
7. The need for anonymity
8. The need for fakes and forgeries
9. The need for rejuvenation
10. The need for playing at hard work

There are, of course, many other needs which you may discover. Some are to a certain extent overlapping. As you read this chapter, you will see how others capitalized on these needs and discovered new ones to make them rich.

THE J.'S GOOD LIFE

Monty and Suzanne J. have led the good life for years since they established themselves as column "planters." Column planters fulfill a need for recognition. They send tidbits of information about celebrities and would-be celebrities to newspaper and magazine columnists. There is no guarantee that the items will be used. They frequently are used, though, simply because columnists can't be everywhere at once and they require lots of information to fill their columns. It helps if the column planter knows several columnists or their secretaries personally, but it's not essential. Interesting items seem to get placed in one column or another.

Monty and Suzanne are hired or retained by press agents, publicity firms, major businesses, movie and theatrical producers, and by individuals who want publicity. The J.'s handle about a dozen clients at any one time. Some of these are ambitious young entertainers who pay $2,500 a year to get their names dropped in the right places. Others are business people, authors, politicians, jet-setters and society folk who pay up to $1,000 a month. Together, the clients give Monty and Suzanne an average monthly income of $4,500 after all expenses are covered. Expenses are high for night-clubbing, first-nighting, and partying, but it's a lifestyle the J.'s love. Can you blame them?

Not all column planters earn as much as Monty and Suzanne. Sometimes they are paid on the basis of published insertions at the rate of $25-100 per publication. In other instances they are salaried employees of public relations or press agent firms, earning $12,000 or more annually.

MINDY N. PROFITS FROM PACE-SETTING PARTIES

Mindy N. is a professional party-planner. She helps the rich and the super-rich throw pace-setting parties. Breakfasts, brunches, luncheons, cocktail parties, buffets, smorgasbords, dinners, midnight suppers, weddings and other special occasion celebrations are all money makers for Mindy. Her services include developing a theme; planning a menu, decorations, flowers and special effects; creating and mailing invitations to the guest list, and recording returns; providing at least one culinary masterpiece especially for each party; preparing all of the food and beverages; rentals of china, glass and other necessary furnishings and supplies; setting up and taking down; service before, during, and after the event; and anything else that might be required.

Mindy's income derives from many sources. In the beginning she just took a stab at a fair price. If someone wanted to keep within a budget of $5, $10 or $25 per person, Mindy worked to keep within that budget and still make a profit. Today her cost accounting is more precise. She has worked out a varied menu selection and an ingredient list for each item. Her cost for ingredients is tripled when she estimates the client's costs. Thus, if she estimates her ingredient costs at $100, the base charge to the client will be $300. Wine and liquor are also charged at three times cost. Labor charges for kitchen help, delivery people, waiters, waitresses, and clean-up people are calculated at twice what Mindy pays.

The difference between costs and charges is about half profit. The balance covers business operating expenses such as gas and electricity, depreciation and replacement of appliances, delivery expenses, insurance, phone, bookkeeping and accounting fees, employment taxes, etc.

Mindy averages $24,000 a year from her party catering service. But her income doesn't stop there. She receives a commission on all rentals, supplies, decorations, flowers, special effects, talent, entertainment, orchestras, etc., which she orders for a party. The commission runs from ten to fifty percent. If the party is held in a rented facility which she recommends, she also receives a commission from the establishment.

In addition, Mindy has gradually invested in an inventory of unusual china and crystal, flatware, cloths, folding tables and chairs and other party items which she rents to her own clientele and to other caterers. Rental rates range upward from $1.50 per place setting; $1 per table, 20 cents per chair, $2.50 per cloth, and $350 for a 40' x 60' tent. Clients also pay for breakage and loss at prices in line with wholesale replacement costs.

Mindy calls her rental service her built-in retirement program. "When I stop giving parties," she says, "I'll live on the income from my rentals. It brings in $6,000 a year now. Half goes back to build up the inventory. I buy a lot of items at auctions and bankruptcy sales. I also check the government surplus sales lists regularly. Often the first rental fee returns my whole investment."

You don't have to run as comprehensive an operation as Mindy does to develop a profitable business catering to pace-setters. Clive L. earns over $20,000 a year on omelet parties and crepe brunches. Clive uses his house parties to promote sponsors for charity events at which his omelets or crepes are featured.

Leon P. cashed in on the back-to-nature trend by preparing vegetarian buffets for the wealthy. Leon recognized that the secret to pace-setting is developing a "feel" for a trend and capitalizing on it early. You develop a feel by keeping an eye on happenings, events, and circumstances which catch people's imaginations. A presidential trip to the Far East can inspire a spate of oriental parties; a rise in meat prices makes meatless parties trendy even among the rich.

When hostesses know that they can depend on you for something spectacular, something new, or simply something that tastes especially good and is well-served, you will join the ranks of the exclusive, sought after and well-to-do entrepreneurs.

JOHN R. BANKS ON HUMANITARIAN SERVICE

The need to set the pace is what makes people "first-nighters" at theaters, musicals and at supper clubs or night clubs. Combined with the need to be recognized and the need to be involved in worthwhile causes, it leads those who can afford it to become sponsors or patrons of literary, artistic and other cultural or philanthropic projects.

An understanding of these motivations led John R. to a $55,000 a year business as a fund raiser. There are two types of fund raisers. One works for an agreed upon percentage — generally from 25% to 33% of the funds raised. The other — called an ethical fund raiser — works for an agreed-upon fee for time spent in attempting to raise an agreed-upon goal. This fund raising fee can run several thousand dollars a month for the fund raiser who supervises a five or six month campaign to raise a million dollars. The fund raiser usually brings a team which includes a campaign office manager and a publicity writer whose salaries, paid by the sponsor, run $250 — $300 a week. Campaigns for capital funds, i.e., for monies to build new facilities, run from three to six months in most instances. John's firm conducts about eight to ten campaigns a year for hospitals, museums, colleges, boys' clubs, and other not-for-profit organizations.

John moves from campaign to campaign and sometimes conducts several at the same time in different areas. His services include an evaluation of the goal potential and the leadership available to help reach that goal; organization and direction of campaign leadership and volunteers; development and implementation of the campaign office, procedures, practices and record keeping. In ordinary practice, the fund raiser does not actually solicit funds. He or she arranges for the proper members of the volunteer committee to do the actual soliciting. Most important, the fund raiser sets up the system to identify the largest potential givers and to establish meaningful recognition for them.

John does this by meeting with a select committee of the sponsor's board who, with him, reviews the names of wealthy men and women in the area, estimating the gift they should be solicited for. Sometimes, a group of these names has been developed in the goal potential evaluation which has been accomplished by interviewing a representative sample of the community. Sub-committees are organized to contact the select individuals who in turn are asked not only for gifts but also for names of others who should be solicited. For each campaign, John develops a recognition pattern for donors. The largest donors may have their names or the name of a loved one on the new building or on a wing or unit. Others may be recognized in commemorative plaques to be erected in the institution, or by certificates, plaques or insignia which they may display in their own homes or offices, or by publicity stories, or by a combination of all of these.

John has learned that the most significant factor in successful fund raising is the recognition of the needs of the wealthy. Statistics indicate that between 80% and 90% of campaign totals come from 6% to 10% of the total number of contributors. In recent years, tax advantages for contributors have provided another motive for giving, but most fund raisers agree that the prime motivation for the wealthy is to fulfill the needs for recognition, to be pace-setters, and to be associated with worthy causes.

There are several ways to get started in a fund raising business. One is to work as a volunteer in a capital fund raising campaign for your church, synagogue, hospital, museum, college, or a charity. Another is to work part-time for an established fund raising concern which has undertaken a project in your area. A third way is to study the available books and periodicals in the field until you have developed the confidence to tackle a campaign on your own. Then you can begin to solicit your own clientele. If you take this course and land a campaign, it's a good idea to hire a secretary or office manager who has had experience working in a fund raising office. You can find people in this category by advertising.

FADS AND FASHIONS FOR THE PACE-SETTERS

Pace-setters are the first to pick up a fad or fashion in their own area, among their own society and often far beyond. If you are going to design original costume jewelry, take a leaf from one of the most successful designers and cultivate a wealthy clientele even if you have to give the first piece or two without charge to a pace-setter who will boost you as a personal discovery.

Joanna P., a custom-dressmaker who clears over $30,000 a year selling creations in the $300 — $500 category, conducts free fashion shows for charities in which the rich are heavily involved. Danny W., whose suede and leather jackets and coats are sought out by the affluent, donates several each year to charitable organizations to use as door prizes at their $100 a ticket fund raising functions.

Mollie W., who never finished eighth grade, earns over $10,000 a year designing and applying unusual monograms on clothes, linens, and luggage to personalize the belongings of the rich. Mollie is on call to fashion designers, furriers, and stores which sell linens. While machine application of a traditional monogram goes for only a few dollars, Mollie earns up to $25 for an original design. She also gives package rates when she does many pieces as in a trousseau.

Rudi N. made a quick fortune designing nature jewelry, using feathers, fur, stones, shells, and clay beads to create one of a kind necklaces and pendants which he sells at $40 to $100 each.

Fads in jewelry and fashion can be manipulated by publicity and word of mouth campaigns. Rudi, for example, has not tried to squelch the story that his grandmother was an American Indian. "It's not true," he says, "and I never repeat it. But a lot of rich people have taken up the cause of the American Indian and the story adds a mystique to my baubles."

You can sense the trends of fashions by following prominent designers through newspapers and periodicals. You can visit boutiques, galleries and showrooms. You can study the trends in exclusive department stores or at places where fashionable people congregate. You can also create trends. Fashionable boutique and department store buyers are always on the lookout for attractive new wares. Some hold regular hours, weekly or monthly, to examine new products and designs. Others can be contacted by mail or phone. Buyers will often make suggestions on how your products can be changed to meet their clientele's needs.

Many rich people prefer to purchase what has come to be known as the "comfortable classic." This is something that can be worn season after season without appearing dated. A few of the classics you might find in wealthy wardrobes are the basic black dress, the camel hair polo coat, the trench coat, the blazer jacket for men and women, and the simple string of real pearls. You can be inscribed in both fashion and banking history if you can create *a* classic or sponsor someone who can.

This brings us to a very important bit of advice. You can get rich even if you have no creative talent of your own. You can make your fortune sponsoring, advising, coordinating, promoting, or selling for a creative individual. Your skills in business are as important, perhaps more important, than the creative skills when it comes to making money. Those individuals who are both talented and business-wise have many opportunities to strike it rich. Those who have one skill or talent can develop their opportunities by joining with others who have complementary know-how, or by developing additional abilities which are waiting to be used.

MEYER B. CATERS TO WEALTHY FEET

Meyer B. was a poor immigrant boy when he became a shoemaker's apprentice in the U.S. depression of the 1930's. He was constantly impressed by the rich men and women who brought their custom-made shoes to be repaired. He learned that most of these shoes had been made abroad when their owners were not pinched for funds. He learned, too, that while money for travel was tight, many who had become used to the comfort of handcrafted footwear were still willing to pay for it.

Meyer borrowed $500 from his brothers and sisters and opened his own shoe repair shop. He placed a small hand-lettered card in the window: "LET MEYER CUSTOM-CRAFT YOUR SHOES HERE." By word of mouth, his business flourished till soon he was earning more than he had ever dreamed would be possible even in America. In the depression, those who earned several thousand dollars a year were truly wealthy. Meyer was able to buy a two-family house, raise six youngsters and send them to college, and finally, just a few years ago to retire to a condominium in St. Petersburg, Florida.

The custom-making of shoes has been referred to as a vanishing art. Yet, Barth W., a long-haired unemployed musician, turned his hands to sandal-making and is earning over a thousand dollars a month selling his footwear at craft-shows, flea markets, and fairs. Barth sells his sandals for children, men and women at prices ranging from $15 to $45 a pair, depending on size and type of leather. He learned his craft from an article in a women's magazine which he picked up while waiting for a job interview. "Never read a women's magazine before or since," Barth laughs, "but if I ever need another money-making idea, I might even subscribe."

There is still a lucrative market for shoes which are classic, comfortable and custom made to the customer's special needs. While these shoes sell for a great deal more than store-bought ready-mades, the market is not confined to the very rich. It includes those with orthopedic problems or deformities and also many average income people who have to pamper their feet because they are on them so much. In the latter category, there is a large potential market among waiters and waitresses, barbers and hairdressers, pharmacists and dentists, and professional athletes.

FILLING THE NEED FOR RECOGNITION

The need for recognition goes hand in hand with the need to be a pace-setter. After all, how can one set a pace for anything if nobody else knows about it? The need for recognition, however, goes beyond the pace-setters. Scions of historic families who want to serve their country in political office often retain public relations counselors, press agents and column planters to keep their names favorably in the public eye.

While there is a tendency to gravitate toward major public relations firms whose staffs handle many clients at fees ranging from $10,000 to over $100,000 per year, there is still a great potential for smaller firms or individuals who will devote their efforts to one or several clients. The chief stock in trade of these small firms consists of a typewriter, a mimeograph or offset press, a telephone, and an ability to develop attention-getting promotional ideas, well written news releases and feature stories highlighting their client. In smaller communities, fees range from several hundred dollars to over $1,000 per month. Individuals who take on a potential political candidate work on retainers or salaries ranging from $12,000 to $35,000 annually.

Candidates for state and national public office are not always wealthy on their own, but they generally have large sums available to them from political contributions. The need for recognition is so strong among would-be candidates, that vast sums of money are spent to fill this need. You can capitalize on this in many ways.

Campaigns for public office, either to secure the nomination or to win the election, can use both generalists and specialists. As the population becomes more visually oriented, there is increasing need for television production. Sensitive and creative producers, script writers, photographic crews, sound-crews, make-up artists, film editors, etc. are all needed, generally on a free-lance basis. There is always a need for a fresh, new, dynamic approach.

The campaign is a mammoth undertaking and provides many opportunities. The role of the campaign coordinator is of prime importance. It requires astute administrative abilities as well as a political understanding. Campaign financing requires a specialist who can supervise the fund-raising as well as the spending program. This position can be filled by someone with a knowledge of the campaign laws, a background in business, law, or accounting, and a strong concept of fund-raising. Speech writers, graphics people, advance men to create and develop enthusiasm for special appearances as well as to make sure that the facilities are adequate and press coverage stimulated, appointment secretaries, etc., are all necessary in a well-run campaign.

Breaking into this field can be accomplished through contact with the county chairman of the political party or through a party committeeman or woman. Direct correspondence with potential candidates, even before they are designated, has also been successful. In some instances, you can even encourage someone to consider a candidacy and then promote that candidacy within the party.

GHOSTS WHO LAUGH ALL THE WAY TO THE BANK

Celebrities in many fields and wealthy men and women who have interesting memoirs often seek further recognition or money through publication of autobiographical materials. In some instances these people are sought by publishers who believe that they can profit from a book by a big name.

While many who have led interesting lives can write interesting stories, few can produce a well constructed book for the mass market. To fulfill the latter function, ghost writers are often engaged either by the "author" or, sometimes, by the publisher.

Occasionally a book by a famous name will carry that name and the ghost writer's. Generally, however, the ghost writer does not have his or her name on the published book, though it may appear as a credit.

The function of the ghost writer varies with the individual job. In one instance it may simply be to rewrite or to rearrange material previously written by the "author." In another, it might be to write the book from scratch.

Payment varies, too, and is negotiable. It can be a flat fee, based on time involved or on guestimates of the possible royalties. Or, it can be a contractural share of the royalties. Flat fees can range from $1,000 or $1,500 to $10,000 or more. Royalties, which are generally 10% of the selling price of hard cover books, are generally split between the ghost and name author. The ratio of the split should be negotiated in advance and agreed upon in writing. Rights to soft cover editions are either sold outright for fixed sums of money or are published on a royalty basis, often 6%. The ratios of ghost and name author splits in these instances, too, depend on advance negotiation and agreement. In most cases, a ghost may request and receive an advance against fees or royalties.

You may make contacts through classified ads in literary magazines, book review sections of papers and periodicals, and through direct solicitation of publishers, literary agents, and celebrities. If you have an idea for a book based on a particular person's experiences, it is worthwhile to contact the individual directly. You will be more apt to receive a favorable response if you have some indication of a publisher's interest.

Many wealthy people will pay not only to have a book written in their name but also to have it published. Self-publication can be accomplished through the so-called "vanity press." You will find "vanity press" publishers advertising in most literary media. Should you be unable to contact a publisher who will undertake this kind of venture, you might solicit area printing firms to do the job. The latter route is more time consuming for you, a fact which should be reflected in your fee.

SELLING TO THE VERY RICH

If a salesman were to receive a commission of one percent on sales and sold an item at $100 per unit, he'd have to sell a thousand items to earn $1,000. If, however, he sold an item at $1,000, he'd only have to sell one hundred items to make the same $1,000. While the market for more costly items is not as extensive as the general market, there is nevertheless a huge potential for building big bank accounts filling the material needs of the wealthy.

You do not have to stick to one product or service. You can seek out a number of non-competitive lines to represent simultaneously. You will be on the look-out for high price-tag items which will meet the special needs of people who can afford them. Among these items are airplanes, helicopters, custom autos, sailboats and yachts, country and seaside properties, secluded resorts, furs, jewelry, custom-made clothing, antiques, paintings and sculpture, tennis courts and golf courses, saunas, hunting and photographic safaris and hundreds of other costly items.

It is helpful to have an extensive knowledge of the fields you represent, but it is not essential. It is more important to develop wide contacts in the market and to be a good salesperson. When you find a decisive interest in a product you represent and you need help in clinching the sale, the manufacturer will generally provide people with precise expertise to help you.

You do not have to represent major manufacturers to strike it rich. You can feather your nest as Sanford D. did, representing serious artists and craftspeople. Sanford recognized that the artistic temperament is not always practical or business oriented. He frequented art and craft shows, soliciting those creative people whose products ranged upwards of $100 in price. He persuaded these artists, sculptors, woodworkers, weavers, etc., to let him represent them for a fee of 25% on items in the $100-$500 category and 33% on those above $500. Sanford solicited architects and interior decorators, showing slides of the artists' works and offering to have original designs executed. In his first year as an artists' and craftsmen's representative, Sanford cleared $9,500. His average income now runs more than twice that, much of it coming from repeat customers.

Custom crafted or individualized items can be priced at what the traffic will bear. There is generally little relation between the cost of labor and materials of designer originals and the actual selling price. In fact, line for line copies or reproductions often sell for a mere fraction of the original cost. What the wealthy pay for is often just exclusivity, the limited edition, the first or one of a kind.

Baron Arnaud de Rosnay invented a new game called "Petropolis." A New York department store carries a deluxe edition of the board game. An exclusive version of the game has a hefty price tag of $790 and comes in a leather lined case and includes silver and gold plated playing pieces in a small leather purse. Newspaper articles commenting on the game noted that heads of state have ordered quantities of the exclusive version and that an even more expensive limited edition package was planned. A popular version of the same game, which adapts the principles of the famous Monopoly game to play-dealing in oil, is projected to sell at $16.

The baron, who knows and understands the wealthy market because he is part of it, obviously recognizes that selling to the very wealthy requires a different mind-set than selling to the general market. While many of the richest people in the world are very conservative — sometimes frugal with their money — and while none of them like to be "taken" — they can afford to and do indulge their whims and fantasies at costs that might seem outrageous to many of us.

FILLING THE NEED FOR FAKES AND FORGERIES

We have already noted the market for copies of designer originals in women's fashions. Celia S. took her family out of the depression doldrums because she could look at a dress selling for hundreds of dollars in Saks or Bergdorf Goodman and then copy it exactly, tailor it to a perfect fit, and charge less than half the original price. Celia's clientele brought her their own fabric and happily paid $100 for her workmanship on a dress. Though Celia worked on an old-fashioned treadle sewing machine in a corner of her apartment bedroom, her average income often exceeded $1,500 a month and her children were the best dressed in school. "My children are great advertisements for me," Celia pointed out.

"When people ask them where they got their beuatiful clothes they tell them about me and my work. I've never had to advertise because one customer recommends another and I have more work than I can handle by myself."

In a small city in upstate New York, Dominick L., a recent Italian immigrant who had apprenticed to one of the famous design houses in the old country, opened a custom men's clothing shop before he could even speak English. Trading tailor-made garments for an advertising campaign, Dom has succeeded in attracting a clientele of physicians, legislators, business executives and wealthy young men who enjoy fine quality fit and can afford to pay for it. $300 is the basic charge for a three piece suit which includes either a vest or a second pair of trousers. Sports jackets at $175 have attracted many clients. Originally located in a small store with an apartment behind it for his family, Dominick has now moved to a larger store in which he carries fine lines of manufactured men's wear, and he and his family live in a recently purchased farmhouse which "reminds us of the old country — only is so much bigger."

Copies of art and jewelry pieces are also in great demand. So are reproductions of rare antiques and period pieces. The latter are often needed by museums or historic restoration projects as well as by architects and interior decorators commissioned by wealthy clients. There is a rich market for authentic copies of period pieces in wood, pewter, silver, gold, vermeil, bronze, tin, pottery, china and stained glass. There is also a need for reproductions of original fabric designs and textures for upholstery and draperies. To get started in this business, you might canvass the museums, restoration projects and historic societies in as wide an area as you can cover. You will find the personnel helpful and generous with advice. You will be able to learn which pieces offer the greatest interest for reproduction buyers, which pieces the project itself is considering for reproduction, which architects, decorators and homeowners are especially interested in period pieces, and what prices are currently being paid for the copies. When you are ready to sell your services, you should have representative samples of your work available or color slides showing attention to fine detail. If you can afford to donate a desired reproduction to a museum, you will generally receive a great deal of word-of-mouth publicity among potential purchasers.

If you are dealing with modern works, extreme care must be taken to avoid infringement on copyrights, design patents and other proprietary interests. Regardless of the age of the original, care should be exercised to assure that your work will not be misrepresented as the original rather than the copy that it is. Several techniques may be useful. One is to prepare an accurate description of your work as a copy or reproduction and to include this description on your bill of sale and buyer's receipt or purchase acknowledgment. Another is to inscribe your name, initials, or trademark and the date inconspicuously somewhere on your product where it cannot easily be removed. It may sometimes be difficult, but is is vital to determine that your work will be used for legitimate purposes only. Legal advice for protecting your interests should be sought if there is any doubt about the right to reproduce a work or about the purpose of the client in commissioning the reproduction. Needless to say, you must carefully rule out any work which is designed to defraud any unwitting buyer who may be led to believe that the copy is the real thing.

FILLING THE NEED FOR PLAYING AT HARD WORK

For nearly every socialite who thinks it's fun to run a charity bazaar, banquet or ball, there's likely to be a hard-working back-up organization which handles the myriad of arrangements while the chairperson takes the bows. The most successful of these events are carefully engineered and orchestrated by professionals who seek out influential, wealthy or celebrity "names" to serve on "the committee."

In actuality, it is fun to set up a miniature empire or organization, to chair an elegant or exciting event, to raise lots of money for a worthy cause, and to receive the plaudits of the press, family and friends for a job well done. It satisfies the need for recognition, the need to be a pace-setter, the need to be identified with an accepted concern, and the need to play at hard work. Although attitudes are beginning to be less rigid in many circles of the very wealthy, it is not generally considered *de rigueur* to do hard work.

Filling these needs presents a myriad of opportunities.

You can create an organization which will do all of the leg work and implementation required for profitable and striking charity events. One firm of this type works with the sponsors to select and persuade socialities or people of influence to chair the committee. The next step is the development of lists of potential ticket purchasers or contributors. This is usually done by having each committee member submit a list of people who "should attend" or can be influenced to attend. The influence of social or business obligations is used liberally. Following up the invitees and converting them to attendees is another function of the committee which is often laid off on the professional planning firm. The firm generally also handles the publicity, fund collections and disbursements, record keeping, arrangements for printing menus, programs and seating lists if they are to be used and serves as liason with the hotel, restaurant or caterers who are handling the event.

Fees for such a project run from $2,500 to upwards of $10,000 plus secretarial and out-of-pocket expenses. It is generally believed that a time span of three months is necessary from the beginning of the planning to the conclusion of the project. However the initial stages require only part-time attention or involvement, and the period of time between the mailing of the invitations to the return of a heavy flow of responses is relatively free. The last two or three weeks are usually full of frenetic and hectic activity and pressures. Working within this time framework, a well organized individual with a competent secretary can handle six projects a year giving personal attention to each. In order to undertake more projects or to do extensive travel nationwide between project sites, additional secretaries with executive talents are necessary.

Fund raising events are not the only efforts in which the wealthy play at hard work. Serving as chairpeople of prestigious panels and commissions is another means by which individuals can be catapulted into prominence in the public eye. While many chairpeople have genuine interest and background in the subject area of the panel or commission, others, not quite as qualified, seek or are asked to serve to fill special needs of political, social or business groups. Panels and commissions generally require sophisticated expertise to research and analyze the issues at hand and to prepare reports and recommendations. There is a need in these groups for paid specialists to serve as consultants and administrators, research assistants, statisticians, legislation drafters, public information liasons, etc.

FILLING THE NEED FOR MONEY MANAGEMENT

When Nelson A. Rockefeller appeared before the Congressional committee investigating his background prior to his appointment as Vice-president of the United States, many people were surprised to learn that, despite the family's vast wealth and involvement in some of the major industrial and financial organizations in the world, the family engaged financial advisers in both consulting and managerial capacities.

Others not quite as rich need and can afford such help. The need is particularly acute among theatrical and entertainment figures whose income potential in their fields may be large but of sporadic nature. While the theatrical or entertainment or literary agent may undertake financial management in addition to services in "selling the product," or management firms may perform some of the functions of the agent, it is generally beneficial for the artist to engage the functions separately. The artistic temperament is often difficult to work with, but many people have found that it is possible and profitable to share the fortunes of a rising star or stars.

The entry into this business is facilitated by association in the milieu of the entertainer or artist; by placing and responding to ads in the related periodicals; and by direct contact. While the potential for income is greater in handling an established personality, getting established in the business often requires nurturing comparatively unknown but talented individuals or groups and growing with them.

Law firms and accountants as well as bank trust departments are often sources of referrals for other wealthy people who require assistance with their day to day handling of funds and investments. Another door to the field is often through response to ads for a personal, confidential or executive secretary.

Explicit in the background requirements along with skill and acumen in financial matters is the ability to withstand a rigorous character and financial investigation. In some instances, bonding is also required.

CAPITALIZATION ON THE WEALTHIEST WOMEN'S NEED FOR MONEY

Gossip columnists have had a field day following the trails of some of the world's wealthiest women to the resale or thrift shops where they exchange hardly worn fashions for cash.

The resale shop buys at a fraction of the original cost, usually marks-up by at least 100% and still provides a bargain for discriminating shoppers. Resale shops which deal in the most fashionable furs and other garments are often located discreetly in fashionable shopping areas. Some are less discreet and extensively advertise both their buying and selling services. Some arrange for pick-up of clothing from prestigious women who are temporarily in need of cash or from those whose wardrobe closets have grown too crowded. Others require delivery to them and will arrange for privacy by appointments, by separate entrances for buyers and sellers, or in some cases completely separate locations.

Even though shops of this type sell real bargains, prices are not low except in comparison to those for originals. So it is not surprising that many customers are also wealthy people who relish a bargain. Other customers include aspiring actresses and career women whose requirements or tastes for high fashion clothes exceed their pocketbook.

It was once thought that shops such as these were economically feasible only in the larger cities, but this is no longer true. Thrift or resale shops in suburban areas have become extremely successful and those in resort or tourist areas are most lucrative. In some instances, the shops have expanded to include antiques, bric-a-brac and objects d'art in addition to clothing.

There is competition from the not-for-profit sector to be considered before opening such a shop, particularly in a suburb or small city. While there are many people who will sell their discards, there are many more who prefer to give them to a charitable institution and receive either the satisfaction of giving or a tax deduction or both. As a result, hospital auxiliaries, Junior

Leagues, and other similar organizations run new-to-you shops as fund-raising efforts. This competition should be thoroughly and objectively evaluated before a profit-seeking enterprise is begun in the same neighborhood. Just because competition exists, however, does not necessarily rule out a successful business. Some resale shop owners regularly add to their inventory by selective purchases from their nonprofit competitors.

FILLING THE NEED FOR ANONYMITY, PRIVACY AND PROTECTION

While many jet setters thrive on publicity and public acclaim, many more of the super rich seek to avoid the public eye as much as possible. While this partially can be attributed to personal, emotional attitudes, there is certainly also a consideration for the security of property as well as family members.

When Ben J. returned from service in Vietnam with only one arm, he found it difficult to get a job. Deciding to go into business for himself, he investigated the field of burglar alarm systems. He found several concerns from which he could purchase systems as he needed them, and he hired a former army buddy to do the installation. Living in a resort area, Ben first solicited area businesses, then well-to-do residents and finally wealthy vacation home owners. His first year brought profits beyond all expectations. Since then he has been personally clearing about $18,000 a year. In addition to soliciting business and home owners, Ben works with architects and builders who incorporate his security systems within new homes.

Marty R. chose another security area to provide security for his family when a heart-attack forced early retirement from his industrial job. He recruited a roster of husky young men and women, and organized a business to provide bodyguards and security personnel for individuals, businesses and institutions. His staff is carefully screened and covered by bonds. Staff members also receive training to adequately handle their jobs which can include serving as a gate-guard on a huge estate or chauffering a young heiress to and from her various engagements or keeping the crowds away from a successful rock star.

There are as many paths to riches as there are rich people's needs. The only tolls you pay to start up these paths are RE-SEARCH; IMAGINATE; CONTACT; and HONING IN. If you need a further incentive to find your fortune filling the needs of the wealthy, remember that the folk saying "Money goes to money" also works in reverse "Money comes from money."

5

BANKING ON THE NEEDS OF BUSY PEOPLE

IDENTIFYING THE CATEGORIES OF BUSY PEOPLE

Who are the busiest people you know?

Why are they busy?

What do they have in common?

Are they typical of their colleagues in particular careers or fields of business?

Answering these questions starts the process of analyzing the needs of busy people. As you establish the broad categories into which these individuals fit, a pattern of needs emerges. You can make this pattern produce profits for you as it has for thousands of others.

Let's take a few examples. Industry executives, professional practitioners, politicians and housewives with families are generally busy people. In most cases, they always have more to do than they have time to do it in.

If you could package time and sell it by the ton, you could live on Easy Street forever. But, even if you cannot sell time as if it were steel or coal, you can still get rich selling time-saving products or services. Or you can sell products or services which busy people cannot find time to make or do for themselves.

ANALYZING THE NEEDS OF BUSY PEOPLE

The prime need of busy people is in the time saving — or time expanding-field. It is possible to subdivide this into special needs categories. We can project some of these categories from our own experience. Additional insight comes as we observe or imaginate the lives of busy people we know or read about.

We can start with the basic needs — food, shelter and clothing. The convenience food industry is built upon the needs of busy people who no longer have the time nor the resources to raise and prepare their own foods from scratch. As for housing, few busy people have the time to build their own, or to physically maintain the complex appliances, fixtures and systems in most households. They have no time to paint the walls, clean the windows, restring the venetian blinds, reupholster the furniture, thoroughly clean the carpeting, refinish the floors or even to clean their attics, basements, and closets. Nor do busy people have the time to make their own clothes, to alter those they buy, or, in some instances, even to shop in the conventional manner for their own needs or for gifts.

All over the country successful businesses have grown to fill these needs and opportunities still abound.

When Carla T. lost her lucrative job with a public relations agency, she developed a mail-order lingerie service catering chiefly to the busy women in the skyscraper office building where she had worked.

"Somehow," she noted, "most career gals have to make time to shop for a dress or a coat, but buying lingerie takes almost as much time as shopping for anything else, so it often gets put off. It's really much taster to order by mail with a satisfaction guarantee."

Carla canvassed a half dozen lingerie manufacturers to arrange for her inventory and sent out photos of new lines to all of the secretaries in the office building. She filled the orders from home. By including additional order blanks, each mailing served a number of people in the same office. The technique Carla used to develop a mailing list is worth noting. She went into the building lobby, photographed the directory of tenants and had the photograph enlarged so that it was clearly legible. Then she addressed an envelope to "Secretary" for each firm. The new business has gone so well that Carla is now putting on help and still clearing $5,000 over her salary as an employee.

Carla's experience is just one example of a success story filling a basic need of busy people. There are countless others. There are needs, moreover, beyond the basic ones. Just for starters, consider the need for relaxation; the need to keep physically fit; the need to fulfill social obligations; the need to participate in community, civic, service or professional organizations; the need for additional education; the need to keep up with current developments in one's field; or even the need to get up on time.

MARGE'S MERRY MORNING WAKE UP

Widowed at 55 and without any vocational skills, Marge W. needed to earn several hundred dollars a month to meet her basic needs. She advertised a "merry morning wake up service" in the personal column of the daily newspaper. Within two months she was phoning 120 people each morning between six and eight a.m. and another 25 at assorted times during the day. She set her rate at $3.00 per month for five calls per week and charged $5. for a wake-up and call back service for those who tend to go back to sleep after the initial call.

"I was surprised to discover how many people preferred the phone to an alarm clock or radio alarm," Marge told us, "but I found that many people need a human voice to get them started in the morning."

Marge also learned that it takes about 20 seconds to dial and announce the time. By advising her clients that she would be scheduling her calls from fifteen minutes before the required time to ten minutes after, she was able to handle the peak hours for the service. ·

FILLING THE EXECUTIVE'S NEED TO KNOW

Executives in every field need a great deal of information to stay abreast of current and projected developments which may affect them.

Among their information needs are:

1. Technological developments
2. The money market
3. How to minimize taxes
4. Competitive products and services
5. Trends in marketing, advertising and sales promotion
6. New laws, regulations, policies and interpretations
7. Changing personnel in the field
8. Management techniques
9. Sociological and demographic changes
10. Political implications.

There are hundreds of articles written each month on subjects which can affect each business, industry and profession. There are relevant trade journals and magazines, technical publications, and books. There are films, plays, news stories and radio and television productions which might be relevant.

To peruse each of these vehicles for new information takes something the busy individual does not have — time. Yet the need to know cannot be ignored.

TRISHA L. TEACHES EXECS TO BEAT THE CLOCK

Does $35,000 a year sound like a decent income? You can earn that much, and much, much more if you capitalize on the "need to know."

Trisha L. did. She expects to make twice that this year teaching speed-reading to executives. Public classes are held in a meeting room of a shopping center or an area motel. Special classes are held for groups of executives from a single company. These are taught in a company meeting room, on company time and on company money. Such groups are charged 10% less per person than the public individual fee of $250. The fee covers eight two hour classes. Public classes are offered in the evening on a Monday-Wednesday, Tuesday-Thursday schedule or for four hours on Saturday morning or afternoon.

How did Trisha get started mining this gold? She answered an ad and took a speed reading course herself. Then she taught a few friends the process. When she decided to make extra money at it, she placed a small ad on the business page of the newspaper.

"I invested $56 in that ad," she recalls. "I also paid a $25 deposit to reserve a meeting room. I remember thinking that if I only got one answer I'd be ahead."

Trisha's first class consisted of eight students. She now averages 24 and usually requires an assistant at classes of this size. Today, clients come through direct mail campaigns, business page advertisements and by referrals. Trisha spent over $10,000 on sales promotion last year, much of it to open new markets. Meeting space rental ran $12,500 and travel expenses $7,500. Assistants, usually college students, were paid $3.00 an hour, for a total of $9,600. Several assistants, now college graduates, have been trained to serve as full time speed-reading teachers for Trisha's new clients.

You can learn speed-reading techniques just as Trisha did. You may find that the course is being offered at low cost at some nearby college or you may take the course in a commercial speed reading program. You may also represent a franchised speed reading organization.

Teaching executives how to save time reading may be your route to money-country. Or, your passport might lead you to riches via another OPN route. You can develop a means of transmitting information in an abbreviated, easy-and-quick-to-absorb fashion. One of the vehicles you could use is a newsletter or a digest.

HOW TO CREATE A PROFITABLE NEWSLETTER

A newsletter or digest can be as simple as one sheet of paper mimeographed or printed on one or both sides. It is usually no larger than two sheets or four pages, though in special circumstances supplements may be added. It summarizes, as briefly as possible, current items of interest in any special interest field. The style is generally straight-forward and factual, without embellishment.

Newsletter style is more of a skill than an art. This makes it easy to learn. One of the best ways to learn is to accumulate a file of samples of established newsletters in several fields. Then, study them for style as well as layout and typography.

Newsletters are published weekly, bi-weekly or monthly. Rates vary considerably, from several dollars to several hundred dollars per year. Rates depend, in addition to basic costs, on the size of the market and its ability to pay; the complexity of the material and the sources from which it originates; and to some extent on the intrinsic value of the information. Consultants' newsletters invariably bring higher rates, particularly when they deal with investments or with employment opportunities. Another consideration is whether the fee is to be paid by the individual personally or by the firm. In the latter instance the rate can be somewhat higher.

The cost of producing a newsletter depends on the cost of background information — subscriptions to the various magazines, journals, papers, books and other sources required to keep up to date in the given field; the cost of any additional help you might require to read and capsulize the information and to type it ready for reproduction; the cost of paper and reproduction; processing, addressing and mailing; postage; advertising and other fixed expenses.

Newsletters are sold chiefly by direct mail or by ads in trade or professional journals. Lists for most classifications are available from mailing list or direct mail firms. Often associations in the field will provide mailing lists of their membership for a fee, or will publish directories which can be purchased or secured through a member.

Usually it is wise to do a pre-publication mailing or advertising campaign to determine the degree of interest. Alternatively the first issue may be sent to the entire potential list of purchasers as a free sample. Introductory offers are generally made. These might be a lower rate for pre-publication or charter purchasers, or a gift or gimmick, or a special supplement covering a current interest area.

In selecting a field for a profitable newsletter, one should consider the size of the potential market and its spending power; the degree and quality of competition; the degree of expertise necessary to extract information and communicate it; and the potential for diversification into other profitable areas in the same field.

The fact that one or more newsletters are already published in a particular field should give pause for consideration, but should not, of itself preclude a new venture. It is often possible to develop a different slant or emphasis, or to focus in on a special area of information. Indeed, if there are several newsletters in a field, a valuable contribution to busy people might be a newsletter digest.

You can learn a great deal about opportunities in newsletters from a subscription to Hudson's *Newsletter of Newsletters,* Rhinebeck, N.Y.

PHILLIP W. SUCCEEDS WITH SEMINARS

Phil W. was earning $14,000 as a computer programmer when he realized that many executives or their firms were paying several hundred dollars plus transportation and lodging costs for workshops and seminars presented by experts. Today, Phil directs a seminar service which brings him several times his previous income. Best of all, he is his own boss because he recognized that the need for expert knowledge is acute.

Phil began by offering one day seminars on various phases of electronic data processing (which is what a computer does). He charged $125.00 for the first registrant from a firm and $75 for each additional registrant. He's branched out into other management seminars and often takes his "show" out on the road, presenting the same program in various locations throughout the country.

Workshops or seminars run from one to three days. Subjects are presented by recognized experts or by people who have had extensive experience in the field.

You do not have to be an authority yourself to run a profitable seminar. You do have to know how to assemble a team of experts. This can be done in several ways. One is to secure prestigious sponsorship for the seminar. Another is to offer compensation to those you feel would attract wide audiences. Still another is to assemble a team of experts who would, with you, cooperatively sponsor the program and share in the proceeds.

The financial arrangements with the sponsor depends on the degree to which the program fulfills his needs. A college or university may become a sponsor to promote its image as a prestigious educational center or to bolster enrollments in its continuing education department. A trade or professional association might sponsor a program as a service to its membership or to attract new members. A publication might sponsor a seminar to develop an advertising base. Hotels, motels, conference and convention centers may undertake a series of programs simply to sell rooms.

Depending on the sponsorship and the degree of promotion of the program, experts can be secured for rates ranging from an honorarium of $25 to $100 plus expenses to established lecture rates of several hundred to several thousand dollars. If the program is sponsored by an educational institution, an association, or a publication, members of the staff are often recognized authorities in the field. If they are not, they can recommend those who should be contacted. A source of free expertise is the business enterprise which caters to the field since the seminar will provide a forum to promote its products or services.

Once the sponsorship and the expertise is arranged for, a site must be decided upon. The factors to be considered are costs, to you and the potential attendees; accessibility by air or auto; and attractiveness of the location. Usually the costs of meals, lodging and transportation are separate from the cost of the program itself, though you can negotiate some extra profits from these sources.

Having established your costs for assembling the program and for projected promotional costs, you can determine your rates by dividing the minimum anticipated attendance into your total costs and multiplying by a factor of at least two. The resulting figure gives you a base to adjust to a round figure and to move upward or downward to stay in line with other similar programs.

Minimum lead time for a successful event is four to six months, though established annual programs can be more effective if there is a continuous publicity build-up. After you have developed the printed promotional material for your seminar, the object is to build attendance through advertising, including direct mail, and publicity to all possible media which communicate in anyway with your potential audience and through tie-in promotions. Thus if you were conducting a seminar on photography as it relates to any given field, you would contact all manufacturers of photographic equipment and supplies for free demonstrations, giveaways, displays, or even for purchase of exhibition space.

Publicity to all media should be sent on a planned schedule. In addition to media, all organizations and trade and professional groups identified with the field should be on the routine mailing list. Publicity should include the initial announcement and program overview, photos of the site, photos and background on the participants, "teaser" information on program content, reports on anticipated attendance, and anything else that might prompt people to send their money in.

Direct mail advertising and application forms should be sent as early as possible and a follow-up mailing should be sent several weeks before the deadline. Another successful technique is a telephone follow-up or the use of Western Union Mailgrams.

Every seminar can bring in additional monies from the sale of transcripts, tapes, or other special materials. Peripherally, there are profit potentials in the sale of exhibition space, in photography concessions, and in transportation charters and tours.

TAPPING THE PROFITS IN TAPING

Seminars for professionals and executives have proved to be a bonanza for many enterprising promoters. But, once again, there is the time element which keeps away many who need the seminar information. To capitalize on this, Bob F. created an audio service which tapes seminar proceedings and reproduces and packages the tapes or cassettes. While Bob gets his profits from the seminar sponsors who do the marketing for the tapes and cassettes, others in the field not only handle the production but the sales as well.

If audio production is one of your skills or interests and you can invest in or arrange to rent the necessary taping and reproduction equipment, this can become a dependable source of good income. To build your business you would contact associations and promotional firms which sponsor seminars and business meetings. You can find lists of forthcoming conventions and meetings in such journals as *Meetings and Conventions.* You can also contact hotels and conference centers at which such events are generally booked. While it may be necessary to share some of your income in the latter case, it is often worthwhile to do so in return for the active recommendation of the sales department. Classified advertising under "business services" is another way of promoting this type of business.

While rates can be negotiated on a time or job basis at $25.00 an hour with additional charges for tapes, cassettes and packaging, a more advantageous method is to establish a minimum job rate to cover expenses and to arrange a royalty or commission on all sales.

Tapes and cassettes covering various fields are sold for anywhere from $5.00 for a 12-20 minute popular interest mass market subject to $150 for a set running several hours covering a special interest area. If an organization, association or group does the marketing and you receive a commission or royalty on sales you can continue to reap the rewards of your labors without any additional efforts.

If, however, you are willing to risk the investment in advertising funds and marketing, you can earn bigger dollars developing a seminar or a seminar presentation and selling the tapes directly.

You can also produce tapes on any popular interest subject, particularly in the "how-to" field. "How to Play a Dulcimer," or "Learn to Play a Guitar," or "How to Fix Electrical Appliances" or any one of thousands of subjects. Once again the principles of sound market investigation apply. There must be an inherent need; the market must be economically viable in size, available income, and accessibility by reasonably priced advertising or direct mail; and the cost of securing the basic text or subject matter must be nominal.

HOW TO FILL THE EXECUTIVE'S NEED TO GROW

The need to know is closely associated with the need to grow professionally, to achieve recognition, promotion, or better positions with other firms. While this type of professional growth requires professional knowledge, it also often requires a vehicle or vehicles to achieve social and professional visibility. This explains why many upwardly mobile employees become active in professional, civic, religious, fraternal, or industrial associations.

While ordinary activity in such groups needs only modest time allotments, the position of officer is often an all-consuming task. Jonathan L. capitalized on this by creating a business which you, too, can establish in your own area, designed to handle the time consuming tasks of groups which do not have executive secretaries and to take "farmed-out" projects from those which do. Jonathan's services offer everything an association might need, from minutes, meeting notices and billings for dues and assessments to programs, newsletters, financial statements and annual reports. Other services include publicity, speech writing, fund-raising, outing and conventions. Fees are based on time to set-up the individual association program and to implement it. In some instances a flat annual retainer is established contractually, and billed pro rata monthly. In other cases, fees are billed specifically on projects undertaken during a particular period.

Jonathan's firm grossed $56,000 last year. His average annual retainer was $3,600, with several organizations at $2,500 and others running up to $7,500. For individual projects, his rates are based on $25 an hour plus 1½ times any actual out-of-pocket expenses he incurs for approved services such as stenographic transcripts, printing, mailings, artwork, accounting, etc. Publicity releases run from $75 to upward of $200 depending on the time involved.

MORE OPPORTUNITIES IN THE "NEED TO GROW"

You might also profit from the executive's need to grow by publishing an employment newsletter listing positions in middle management and upper echelons. A subscription at $35 would entitle the recipient to bi-weekly issues for a year. Listings could be secured routinely from businesses throughout the country, from employment agencies and executive research organizations and from the departments of labor in various states.

Another vitally needed business is a relocation service for new employees and those transferred from one part of an organization to another. Generally, the fee would run about $100 per day plus expenses and would be paid by the corporation. The service might include arrangements for packing and moving furnishings, location of living quarters in the new area and, if necessary, setting up the household, arranging for utility hook-ups, household help, charge account applications, school transfers and registrations, and even social introductions to new neighbors and clubs.

MINTING MONEY FROM MEMORY BANKS

The calendar can be your key to a steady income as Kevin McC. learned when he was confined to a wheel chair after an auto accident. Kevin contacted all of the busy people he knew and offered to "remember" the birthdays, anniversaries and other special occasions of their clients, friends and relatives. After receiving the lists of names, addresses and dates, he set them into a calendar file, placing each occasion ten days before its actual date. When the card comes up, Kevin phones the busy executive with a reminder "Your mother's birthday is a week from Friday. You want to get a gift." The card is then advanced to 2 days before the actual date. Once again Kevin phones with a reminder. Friday is your mother's birthday. Did you send a gift?" The basic charge for the two phone calls is two dollars. If on the second call, the executive has forgotten a gift, Kevin will order candy, flowers, plants or other standard items. For the latter service he charges two dollars plus 25% of the cost of the item.

Kevin runs an alternative service for small business people. For a fee of one dollar per name plus costs of cards and postage he will mail birthday and anniversary cards three days in advance of each occasion. He also addresses and mails holiday greetings for those who do not have time to handle their own lengthy lists. Political figures are among his best clients.

Similar in concept to this service is a bon voyage gift service organized by a travel agent alert to opportunities in business needs. For a surcharge of 25%, the agent will arrange to have flowers, candy, liquor, cakes, special diet foods, etc. delivered to a pre-departure traveler on any cruise ship leaving an American port. The agent maintains a photo file of standard gifts available in each port city, and a list of reliable delivery services who will handle special gift pickups and deliveries. In addition to serving area business people, the agent services other travel agencies across the country since these agents frequently find it good public relations to send their cruise customers a bon voyage gift on the day of sailing.

CAPITALIZING ON THE NEEDS OF CAREER WOMEN

Despite the impact of the Women's Lib movement, career women in our society tend to have, more than men, roles which overlap the business world and that of hearth and home. These women, therefore, have additional special needs which offer tempting money-making opportunities.

Picture the life of a 9 to 5 career woman. How does she find an apartment or someone to share the rent? When does she shop or find time to have her hair cut and coiffed? If she has the responsibility for a household and family, what problems are there in feeding, cleaning and ferrying youngsters? What happens when her children become ill? Does she have special esthetic needs?

We have discussed Elmer S's pick-up and delivery service and Carla T's direct mail lingerie business, both of which cater to many career women. You can duplicate their success stories wherever you are. You can also build many more businesses filling the needs of career women.

"EVERYBODY'S UNCLE JACK"

Jack P. is a case in point. He was fed up with daily driving to a dead-end job, and his wife encouraged him to explore a business of his own. But there was little capital to invest, and Jack felt he was too old to learn a new skill.

An assessment of Jack's interests, assets and abilities brought into sharp focus several areas which were obvious but had been taken for granted. Among these were his ability to drive; his well cared for station wagon; his interest in sports; and his love of children. As they discussed the assessment, Jack's wife recalled a conversation among the secretaries in her office. "My son always wants to go to the game on Sunday, but I have to catch up on the housework," one young woman had said. "I have the same problen," commented another. "It's rough being an only parent."

Recognizing the needs of single parents turned Jack P. into "Everybody's Uncle Jack." For a fee of five dollars per child, plus the cost of tickets, Uncle Jack picks up the youngsters, takes them to the football, basketball, baseball or hockey game, and brings home happy youngsters. When his nine seater isn't big enough, Jack rents a jitney which he is planning to buy. Uncle Jack also provides a family-like ferrying service, taking youngsters to the roller rink, their dental appointments, Cub Scout and Brownie meetings and even to visit their daddies and grandparents.

$10,000 A YEAR PLUS ROOM AND BOARD

In effect, Jack is making a living assuming part of the role of a surrogate parent. Shirley and Stanley L. clear two hundred dollars a week as surrogate grandparents. They do not do the general cleaning nor heavy maintenance of a household, but they do take care of the shopping and cooking, the birthday cakes and keeping the cookie jar filled. They help the youngsters with their homework and take them on expeditions and generally bridge the gap between working parents and their youngsters. Like grandparents, Shirley and Stanley come for a "visit" and stay with a family for no less than a week at a time nor longer than a month. Their "regular" families try to book them a year in advance and often change vacation schedules to fit with the "Grams'" calendar. There are never enough weeks in the year to fill the needs. The large, loving family relationship is additional compensation.

SPECIAL DELIVERY LUNCHES FOR LOSERS

Leading a rather sedentary life, required to eat away from home most of the time, and extremely conscious of their appearance, career women seem to have a universal need to control their weight. To fill this need Julio G. takes weekly orders, in advance, for daily fresh vegetable and fruit salads, clear boullions and broths, and daily special luncheons which meet the requirements of the leading dieter's organizations. His rates run from $3.00 to $4.50 per luncheon delivered to the office. Food is prepared in his apartment kitchen, portioned into disposable plastic dishes, labeled by address, contents and price and packed in hot and cold insulated chests, numbered for order of delivery. Deliveries are made from a Volkswagon van parked in a centrally located parking garage. Julio averages 450 lunches per week on which he nets approximately $300. "Not bad for a high school dropout, is it?" asks Julio.

MURRAY K'S CHOW CHOW TRUCK

Catering to the need for prepared meals to be served at home, Murray K. outfitted a step-up truck with refrigeration, steam table and deep-frying equipment. He arranged with a Chinese food restaurant supplier for a dependable source of prepared egg rolls, lobster rolls, and shrimp rolls, an assortment of chow-mein specialties, and fortune cookies. Murray travels a 25 mile circuit covering apartment complexes, suburban developments, school and college campuses, and construction sites.

Murray spent $350.00 to equip his truck, purchasing used equipment from an area hotel and restaurant supply company. He invested $750.00 as a down payment on a used truck, financing the balance of $4,000.00 over a three year period. His average weekly take-home generally exceeds $400.00.

CONVENIENCE FOODS ARE FOOD FOR THOUGHT

Although prepared foods cost considerably more than those made from scratch, the market for them increases as more women join the working force. There are, therefore, continuing opportunities in this field. These opportunities fall into several categories.

One is the preparation of foods for distribution through established supermarkets, specialty stores, or even restaurants. Success stories are rampant about individuals and families who built a fortune from a special sauce recipe or one for home-baked bread.

Another category is that illustrated by Julio and Murray in meals or foods delivered to the point of consumption. Diet foods and dietetic ones, foreign flavored and ethnic foods, and the familiar All-American standbys have all proven winners for enterprising individuals. A simple mobile hot dog, hamburger and soda van covering construction sites or college campuses can send a family through college.

A third category is the special order food. Party casseroles or hors d'oeuvres or fabulous desserts; birthday cakes; holiday fruit cakes; edible centerpieces; barbecued chickens or spareribs are just a few items to think about.

If you are considering finding your fortune in food, you must carefully check the licensing regulations which might apply to your business and your area. Requirements vary in different areas, but may include food handling permits, vendor's licensing, registration and inspection of premises and vehicles used for food; and sundry other fees. Your attorney can advise you of the steps you must take to comply with the laws, or you can check with the area health department.

Any aspect of food sales and service can fatten your wallet if it is carefully evaluated using the standards discussed previously in this book. A particular economic factor which must be considered is the seasonal variation in the cost of raw materials. Another is the essential perishable nature of the inventory. Still another is the difficulty of breaking down total costs to the cost of individual servings or packages. None of these considerations, however, are insurmountable. They are simply noted to call your attention to the caution with which you should proceed to assure the success of your venture

HOW TO BECOME A MILLIONAIRE MIDDLEMAN

The busy woman or man depends extensively on others, who may be just as busy, particularly for specialty services which require narrowing a field of decisions to several viable options. For example, an executive might contact an employment agency or executive search group to secure several applicants for a position. Or, a real estate agent would be called upon to present several possible sites for a new office or factory.

You could list dozens of categories of middleman services, most of which require some special expertise. There is a service, however, which only requires vast and varied contacts and the ability to put together some people's needs with other people's offerings. This is often referred to as the finder's fee field. The finder, as his name implies, earns a negotiated fee for bringing together buyers and sellers, investors and those who require capital, and those who require specialized services with those who can perform them. The fee is generally calculated as a percentage of the total transfer, but can be a sliding percentage in extremely large transactions or can be a fixed sum agreed upon in advance. Five percent is a typical finder's fee. Often the percentage goes higher for difficult assignments. Many "finders" earn six figure incomes.

The most lucrative field is generally finding venture capital. Rich profits also abound, however, in locating sources of scarce materials and in disposing of inventories for those who need ready cash. A study of the financial sections of daily and Sunday newspapers, and continuous perusals of "buyer's wants" and "offerings" in the commercial classifieds and in trade journals can begin to stimulate your thinking. Keeping lists of contacts and sources by category and geographic area is a must.

This field requires a persuasive extroverted personality, a strong grounding in finance, and an ability to mediate between the parties involved. The effective mediator comes up with an agreement in which both parties achieve their essential goals, without necessarily securing 100% of what they were seeking. Serving as a middleman in such an arrangement requires the art of compromise developed to a fine degree. Those who develop this art and practice it effectively are recognized and sought out.

TEN BUSINESS IDEAS CATERING TO
THE NEEDS OF BUSY PEOPLE

1. Fill the need to be organized. Become an efficiency expert. Develop sensible systems to organize filing and other office procedures, billing and collections, collections of books and records and even kitchens and closets. One such "expert" is earning $100 a day.

2. Cater to the need for evening services. Have a custom seamstress or tailor at your home every evening from 5 to 9 to take measurements and mark alterations. If necessary, additional work can be farmed out. Convenience services usually add a minimum surcharge of 25% to prevailing rates.

3. Meet the need to keep fit. Offer yoga classes, calisthenics, exercise machines, rope skipping, running in place, etc. Participants should have medical approvals. If necessary, bring in experts to teach. A charge of $2.50 per hour is about average, but you can check prevailing rates in your area.

4. Fulfill the need for upgrading skills. Develop an audio-visual firm specializing in training film strips, slides and films. Average price for a film is $1,000 per minute of running time. Film strips and slides are much less. Check for prevailing area rates.

5. Cater to the need for corporate social gatherings. Establish a service to organize and implement office parties, executive luncheon and dinner meetings and employee picnics, barbecues, and clambakes. If you are more organization oriented than food service oriented, you might arrange to represent area restaurants and other food handling facilities.

6. Profit from the need for shared apartment facilities for single career women and men. Organize a roommate referral service. Advertise an apartment rental classified listings. Charge $25 for matching potentially compatible rent sharers.

7. Organize car pools for daily transportation, business, vacation, convention and shopping trips. Shared auto costs are often less than air travel rates, and many executives don't like to fly. In addition to classifieds, use office and shopping center bulletin boards and inserts for convention mailings. Charge 10% of the commercial transportation fee.

8. Develop an esthetic need fulfillment service. Build a service delivering fresh floral arrangements to executive offices weekly; or to provide indoor "greenscaping" with potted plants you will service and replace periodically; or to develop a company collection of new artists' works; or arrange to refurbish and redecorate offices or public spaces with modern sculpture, wall hangings or wood carvings.

9. Extend the executive need to keep current with a daily

newspaper digest, a la White House. Summarize the leading stories and features of the area newspapers early each morning. Mimeograph copies and deliver to executive desks, for a fee.

10. Reach a large market with a resume writing service. Many people don't know how to put their best foot forward in a resume or how to reproduce one in quantity. A fee of $25 which includes a dozen finished copies is reasonable for the job hunter and profitable for you.

6

FILLING THE NEEDS CREATED BY GOVERNMENT AND OTHER BIG BUSINESS

When Irving S. completed his tour of duty with the U.S. Armed Forces after World War II he came home with an honorable discharge and an idea. Today Irving is the owner of a chain of department stores and a nationally recognized philanthropist. Irving's idea made him rich.

The idea was to help the government dispose of surplus equipment, merchandise and supplies. "Government issue materials were manufactured to meet rigid specifications," he recalls, "and certainly could be used effectively in the civilian market, especially when the price was reasonable."

The price was determined by bidding at surplus sales run periodically by the Defense Department and other government agencies. "You had to take into consideration the cost of moving the merchandise back to your headquarters, the potential market for specific items, the cost of advertising and general business overhead. But the prices these things went for at government sales were extremely low. We tried to stick to items with a general consumer appeal — blankets, foot-lockers, bunk beds, cots and clothing, but we often got carried away on gadgets and widgets for which we had to dream up a use. Surplus parachutes, for example, became fabric bargains because they had so many yards of delicate looking, strong material."

Irving rented an old barn for his surplus sales, but he attracted orders from all over the world by advertising in the Sunday edition of the New York *Times*. Later, he branched into new merchandise bought directly from the manufacturer, built a new building and created the first of his department stores.

Irving's initial success was based on recognition of the government's need to get rid of surplus equipment. That need exists today as it did then. Federal government surplus sales are held periodically by the Government Services Agency at about a dozen regional sales centers throughout the country.

You can receive free information of sales or auctions at various centers by writing to G.S.A., Washington, D.C. 20405, requesting the leaflet "Buying Government Surplus Property." You'll receive a list of the regional centers to which you can write for applications, for notices of product sales in which you might be interested.

Another major source of surplus is still the Department of Defense. Information on auctions, sales, bids, etc. can be secured from D.O.D. Surplus Sales, P.O. Box 1370, Battle Creek, Michigan, 49016.

You can also pick up great bargains for resale from the U.S. Customs Bureau which requires each of its district offices to hold at least one public auction each year. For information write Bureau of Customs, 21000 K Street, N.W., Washington, D.C. for free list of district offices. Then contact the office nearest you and request free placement on the catalog mailing list.

Customs sales generally require cash payments. Items are sold "as is" which means you should take advantage of the pre-sale inspection period to closely examine those you are interested in.

Don't forget your post office as a source of salable items. Regional offices usually run annual or semi-annual sales of all items uncollected, lost or misaddressed. The pieces are usually sold at an auction. If you have an established market for a variety of products, you may be able to pick them up at a fraction of their original cost at these sales. It's worth looking into. Contact your area post office for address and dates of postal sales.

G.S.A. and D.O.D. sales are often by sealed bid, which means you need not be present at the sale. Catalog descriptions are generally complete and accurate. Terms of the sale are spelled out in each catalog or invitation to bid. Sealed bids normally require a 20% deposit. The defense agency also conducts local auctions, and sales at some military installations.

Even when sealed bids are permitted it is advisable to inspect the merchandise you are bidding on. Traveling expense becomes part of your costs. You must also be prepared to transport whatever you buy and to store it until you sell it.

There are, however, many job lots you can purchase for a few hundred dollars or less and bring home in a rented car, van or trailer.

As one old peddlar put it, "If you buy cheap and sell dear, you can still pyramid a small amount of money into a respectable fortune."

FILLING GOVERNMENT'S NEED FOR PRODUCTS AND SERVICES

Just as you can get rich buying *from* the government, you can make a mint selling *to* government agencies. If you're interested, Uncle Sam will help you. The General Services Administration conducts a special service program to generate competition in government contract work. You can often schedule an appointment with a contracting counselor who will advise you how to win a government contract. Write to: Director of Business Affairs, G.S.A., Washington, D. C. 20407.

You can also get lists of government needs and the particular specifications which must be met by contacting the municipal, state or federal agencies to which you'd like to sell.

You may find additional help in publications, free or low cost, from the Small Business Administration, Washington, D.C. 20416, or at one of the nearly 100 S.B.A. regional offices in major cities throughout the country.

The U.S. Department of Commerce is another source which also maintains regional offices. You'll find them listed in the telephone directory under U.S. Government. Check also for help from your state Commerce Department, generally located in your state capitol, with area offices listed in the phone book under your state heading.

Governments need to buy services as well as equipment. Though some services may require large resources of equipment, labor and technical know-how, there are others which require only your intelligence, perserverance and ability to apply what you can easily learn. One of these is grantsmanship.

GETTING RICH WITH GRANTSMANSHIP

Renzo M. just moved his family into a modest $105,000 country home. Renzo earns over $50,000 a year writing grant applications for municipal water treatment and sewerage facilities. Bradley F., whose income is even higher, develops grant proposals for federal funds for housing, employment and various other municipal social welfare projects.

You can do what Renzo and Bradley do. All you really have to know is how the system works.

Many agencies of the state and federal government are empowered to grant vast sums of money to other subdivisions, agencies, schools and universities, institutions and even to individuals. These grants are made for projects in keeping with prescribed goals and objectives. Sometimes the grant is enough to fund the entire project. Sometimes matching funds are required from the project sponsor. In some instances grants from several agencies can be combined. In other cases one source of funding will rule out another.

Most grants involve large sums, frequently hundreds of thousands and millions of dollars. To seek these funds requires a project which fulfills the goals and objectives of the program. The project cannot be vague or defined in generalities. It must be specific and detailed. Moreover, it must be described in a particular format, often with as many as a dozen copies, to meet application requirements. In addition to detailing the project, the grant application may require projections of costs, analysis of cost-benefit ratios, pro-forma financial statements, proposed criteria and techniques for evaluation and, often, additional information.

If special expertise is required, you can seek the help of architects, engineers, accountants and planners who will be required to implement the project when the grant is received. These people may already be retained by the municipality or on its payroll. If they are not, the costs of their services can be added to your fee.

Bradley and Renzo both point out that almost anyone with average intelligence and writing ability can eventually secure a grant for a legitimate project that falls within program guidelines. But, though most municipal leaders, scientists, educators and planners have all the facts and figures at their fingertips, they frequently lack the time and confidence to write a proposal. In some instances, they are not even aware of all of the possible sources of grant money available.

You can locate many of these sources by studying the latest edition of the Catalogue of Federal Assistance Programs which lists the various programs offering funds for particular purposes. Your congressman may be able to send you a copy or you can order one from the Government Printing Office, Washington, D.C. Specific agencies also provide information on their own funding programs and can be of immeasureable help to you in filling out applications, etc.

When you establish a firm to give advice on how to fund projects and help prepare grant proposals and funding applications, you can be highly paid for this service.

Fees are based on an estimate of the time involved, on a percentage of the grant or on a combination of these factors. In many instances fees are contracted for by phases. The first phase covers the estimated time involved in a study. This is called a feasibility study to establish the basis for the proposal and an analysis of available funding sources. Depending on the size of the project and the potential grant, the fee for this study can be estimated anywhere from $25 to $250 per man hour plus out of pocket expenses. Out of pocket expenses such as travel, food and lodging, secretarial costs, printing, etc., can be charged at 1½ to 2½ times cost.

The second phase usually covers writing the proposal, submission of applications and securing the funding. While the charge for these services can also be based on estimated time, it is often based upon a percentage of the total grant. One percent of a million dollars is $10,000. At that rate you don't need to handle many projects each year to make a good income.

You should also be aware that most funding agencies accept consultants' fees as reimbursable expenses. There is a general tendency on the part of project sponsors, therefore, not to quibble extensively over the size of the fee.

You can fill the need for grantsmanship by developing an expertise in a field which flourishes on grants. Or, you can use your selling skills to develop contacts in a field and sell the services of experts and writers whom you will employ.

You will find your major clients among municipalities seeking state and federal assistance, hospitals and medical research organizations and some of the smaller colleges and universities.

JORDAN O. LOST A JOB, GAINED A BUSINESS

Jordan O. loved his job as an assistant principal of an elementary school, but his position was abolished in a budget crisis. Depressed by many interviews in which he was told, "We need your skills, but we simply can't afford them," Jordan turned to freelance educational consulting and grant proposal preparation. As he developed funding proposals for remedial reading programs, in-service education of teachers, bilingual studies, and other special education programs, he wrote into each not only his initial fee but also funds for project implementation and supervision.

Jordan's total retainer for a project ran from $2,500 to $7,500 — far less than the salary of an ordinary teacher and an attractive deal for a Board of Education to consider.

Making contacts among school administrators, formerly his colleagues, he matched his former income in the first year and doubled it the next. He developed a "staff" of free lance consultants from the ranks of still employed administrators. He then borrowed several thousand dollars from his pension fund and arranged for exhibition space at state and regional conventions for administrators and school boards.

In order to promote his image as a consultant, Jordan wrote and submitted articles to professional journals. He placed a small institutional ad in each of these publications. He also contacted architectural firms which specialized in school design, offering to serve as their educational consultant on a project basis.

Jordan was able to repay his pension fund loan in short order. His consulting firm brings him an average net income of nearly $1,000 a week and brings a supplementary income to his staff of freelance advisors.

The educational field is not the only one which needs and engages consultants. Other areas often offer far better fees. Government regulations have created great needs for financial and tax consulting, for example, and for pension and estate planners. These and health facility planning, environmental and pollution control planning and energy conservation are, because of government policies, among the most fertile fields for consulting work. As more consumer interest legislation is passed, the field of consumer consultant to industry will become equally lucrative.

SHELDON S. SELLS SERVICES TO GRANTSMEN

Sheldon S. took another route to riches. He discovered that many grantsmen, either in their own firms or on the payrolls of major institutions need continuous updating on newly available funding sources and changing criteria established by government agencies.

To fill their needs — and his own need to earn a six-figure income — Sheldon developed a monthly four page newsletter which carries a subscription rate of $65 annually. The newsletter carries current information on grant availability, awards which have been made, and reports on who's who in the various government agencies and foundations which process funding applications.

While the newsletter is lucrative, the bulk of Sheldon's income results from the periodic grantsmanship and development seminars he sponsors in various cities throughout the country. His average charge for a two day seminar program (exclusive of lodging and meals) is $285 per person. At that rate, you don't need many registrants to cover costs and turn a pretty penny.

If you think you can't be a consultant because you're not an expert, maybe you're overlooking your talents. When you inventory your background and experience, you may find that you can sell an expertise that you thought was "just common sense."

YOU MAY HAVE EXPERTISE YOU DON'T RECOGNIZE

Consider the experience for example, of Jean L. who has become an "energy consultant." She averages 5 or 6 projects a month at $300 each, advising businesses and industries how to reduce energy costs.

Jean, a frugal housewife, transferred to the business scene her common sense approach to saving energy money at home.

"I grew up," she says "with a father who always reminded me that 'we don't own shares in the electric company'. When I got married, money was always tight and I kept thick file folders of money saving hints. When the energy crisis became nationally publicized I recognized that many businesses and industries really didn't have the practical experience I had developed."

Jean's direct mail approach and periodic newspaper ads bring in a steady flow of clients. "Referrals also bring new clients. In some larger places, my clients save more than my fee in a month or less," Jean states, "just on simple things like hanging insulated draperies on window walls, setting the timers properly, turning off electric typewriters during phone calls and coffee breaks, and lowering the wattage in corridors, rest rooms and other areas that don't require eye-work."

Jean prepared a check list covering all the energy saving procedures she knew or read about. She added ideas from fuel supply, utility, and insulation companies as well as from engineers who specialize in lighting, heating and cooling. The latter group received referrals when major changes were necessary. A complete survey usually takes Jean two days. She takes another day to write up her recommendations and have them typed.

"The interesting thing about being a consultant," Jean says, "is that you generally tell people things they know or should know themselves. When it's written up in a grand presentation from an outside 'authority', it suddenly becomes important enough to do something about. It's a kind of reinforcement for which business men are willing to pay."

DISCOVERING PROFITS IN NEEDS
GENERATED BY GOVERNMENT

We've noted just a few of the needs of government or those generated by it. These include the need to buy services and materials and to sell surplus; the need for funding packages; and the needs for consulting services in various fields affected by government policies or regulations.

The burgeoning bureaucracy in which we live has spawned thousands of other needs.

In his spare time, on an investment of $1,500 for used offset printing equipment. Harry V. earns $18,500 a year selling printed forms to nursing homes and other health related institutions which must report regularly to multiple government agencies.

Harry recognized the need for printed forms to simplify statistical reporting and record keeping.

Sarah D. earns $50 a day every day during January, April, July and October because she recognized the need to know when and where to file the myriad of papers individuals, institutions and industries are required to submit to government agencies.

"My clients are mostly tradespeople," Sarah notes, "plumbers, carpenters, electricians, etc. All these forms make them nervous. Besides, in the time it would take them to fill out the reports, they could be earning several times my fee."

Sarah completes and files quarterly withholding and F.I.C.A. tax returns for small businessmen in her area. She charges each an annual fee of $100 and handles two each day, every day of the month following each quarter. She fills in additional employment tax reports for a modest surcharge averaging $6.50 per hour.

Arthur N. picks up $3,000 in three and one-half months of evenings between January 1, and the April 15 income tax filing deadline. Arthur, a high school shop teacher, charges $10.00 for short form returns with income up to $10,000, adds 1/10% charge for every $1,000 of income above that. Long form personal tax returns average $50 fees. Arthur does three or four short returns or one long form each evening during tax season.

"You don't need to be an accountant," he says. "You do need to be able to read very carefully and to be accurate with numbers on the calculator. You also have to be the strong, silent type. Income tax reports are confidential and if you blab about anyone's income and expenses you're not going to keep your customers or attract new ones."

MAKING MONEY IN DIRECTORIES

The need to know who's who and where to go for specific information or assistance is not limited to ordinary people with ordinary problems. Newspapers and periodicals, lawyers, consultants, advertising and public relations agencies, schools, universities, libraries, researchers and writers, politicians, associations, lobbyists, business interests and even the various branches of government all require this information.

Federal and state governments as well as some municipalities do publish directories, chiefly for internal use. Additionally, public office buildings and large offices in which internal switchboards are used also frequently publish their own directories. You can generally secure a copy of these directories from the governmental unit involved. If you have any difficulty obtaining it, you should request the assistance of your elected representative.

There are many ways of marketing the information in these directories. You can create and sell, for example, lists of these government officials involved in any special interest field; or you can prepare card indexes or mailing labels; or provide a service to periodically list changes of officials and personnel; or you can offer home addresses and telephone numbers of public officials — all of these services are needed and can be profitably sold.

Graeme T. earns enough money to travel six months each year by using government directories for ideas for "did you know" columns and feature stories. "There are thousands of ideas for articles in the *Congressional Directory* alone," Graeme points out. "It lists not only the names of representatives and senators, but also their biographies; committee assignments; administrative assistants and secretaries. It also details agencies, depart-

ments, courts, international organizations; diplomatic representatives; the press, radio and television corps and other per-
tinent information. The book is a gold mine! And, it enables a
writer to fill a need for background information and interesting
tid-bits about our current governing bodies. There's a story in
every agency."

HOW TO HAVE THOUSANDS OF NO COST EMPLOYEES

Even if you do not utilize government directories as money-
makers in themselves, you will find them invaluable resources in
dealing with the government on your own behalf or in representing others. Renzo M. and Bradley F. discovered that government
employees can be extensions of their staffs. You can, too.

Government employees cost you no more than your share of
taxes if they help you within the scope of their authorized duties.
Thus you can receive, for example, bibliographies of material on
a multitude of specialized subjects by writing the superintendent
of Documents, U.S. Government Printing Office, Washington,
D.C. 20402. Or you can secure reams of information on particular
subjects from the agency concerned with the subject. To find the
proper agency look in your telephone directory under U.S. Government and contact the Federal Information Center nearest you. Tell
the advisor at the center what your interest is and you'll be referred
to the agency which can help you.

Government agencies can provide you with investigative services and research, helping you to track down and trace information, develop counseling reports, and even sell products. If, for
example, you want to sell a product or service overseas you'll get
help from the Bureau of International Commerce, Dept. of Commerce, Washington, D.C. 20230. You'll be fulfilling a government
need for a favorable balance of trade when you sell to foreign
countries.

You can get all sorts of consumer-oriented information from
the Consumer Information Center, Public Documents Distribution Center, Pueblo, Co. 81009; publications on various businesses, bibliographies, fact sheets, and management studies from
the U.S. Dept. of Commerce, Washington, or from one of its field
offices in major cities; and the Small Business Administration in

the nation's capital or in its regional offices will provide loans, advice, and free or low cost publications on many business interests.

It makes sense, under any circumstances, to know who your government employees are and where to reach them. It makes special sense if you include them, as you can, on your unpaid staff of advisors.

WARREN P. CASHES IN ON THE CENSUS BUREAU

Warren P. is an industrial consultant whose earnings exceed $100,000 annually. Among the services his firm provides for fees ranging upwards from $75 an hour are sales market research, labor market research, site selection research, and new product test marketing.

Warren and his staff rely extensively on the government's research facilities. The Social and Economics Statistics Administration, which offers a broad range of information, includes the U.S. Census Bureau. Using the demographic information available from this agency, you, too, can be on your way to lucrative consultant's fees. You can secure at a modest cost such books as the *City and County Data Book* and *A Statistical Abstract of the U.S.*, as well as reports on individual states, from the superintendent of Documents.

Many firms seeking to expand or to relocate require studies to enable them to select an advantageous site for manufacturing, management or sales facilities. You can provide a valuable insight into any area using statistics from the Census Bureau or the Bureau of Labor Statistics to show the potential labor force; numbers of people in various age groups; income levels; wage levels; age and value of homes, etc. The background information can be supplemented by material and advice you can get from area chambers of commerce and tourist or trade bureaus, from state labor departments and from regional offices of the state and federal departments of commerce.

While Warren's fees often run close to $1,000 a day, the range of fees begins at approximately half that and generally runs higher when large investments are riding on the ultimate decision. Clients are solicited by direct mail or by advertising in business journals, newspaper financial sections and trade papers. Unless one starts with an established reputation in the field, usually earned by working with a going firm, it's often difficult to secure the first client. It's well worth trying, though, if you're convinced you can do a good job, because once you develop a reputation, people will seek you out.

CUTTING RED TAPE PUT MARCO A. IN THE BLACK

Marco A. left Cuba as a political refugee before he had a chance to finish his college education. Nearly penniless and with no family to turn to, Marco sought the assistance of government agencies for employment, housing, and sustenance. As he went from agency to agency filling out forms, answering questions, and being referred from one to another, Marco discovered a need which solved his financial problems. He discovered that many of his fellow refugees were having even more problems than he. They needed help in getting by the language barrier, getting directed to the proper agencies, and cutting through the red tape of qualifying for assistance on problems of business, education, health and welfare.

Marco, in effect, became an ombudsman for these people. Charging whatever the traffic would bear, sometimes only a few dollars and sometimes a barter of possessions, Marco represented not only his fellow refugees but a whole foreign born population whose difficulty with English made it difficult to deal with government agencies.

The profession of "ombudsman" developed in Sweden. There, the ombudsman — or woman — is an individual whose job it is to serve as the representative for complaints. In this country ombudspeople serve to cut red tape and find answers to complaints and problems. They know how and to whom to go to get things done within the framework of particular agencies and institutions. With a specialty of problem solving, the ombudsperson is usually a generalist with a great deal of tact, persuasive abilities and persistence who knows how to reach through to the top decision maker in any field.

On a small, but nevertheless profitable scale, ombudsman services can be established to meet the special needs of various communities or neighborhoods. These services are especially

needed where there are significant numbers of foreign born resi
dents or large groups of low income families.

These people need services ranging from reading and interpret-
ing letters and answering them, to guidance in seeking business
opportunities and financial assistance. They need, often, to be
told to whom to go for what and how to make their requests. In
many instances they need to have someone clear the way by making appointments and explaining the problem, 'or they need someone to go with them to help them cut red tape and get through to
the proper officials.

Helping secure a small business loan, keeping a youngster from
being suspended from school, finding adequate housing in government sponsored projects, securing necessary public assistance,
etc., are all examples of the kinds of assignments an ombudsman
might undertake. Ombudsmen may also specialize in certain areas.
Specialties might be youth, drugs, environment, education, pov-
erty or minority group problems.

The ombudsman service can be provided on a fee ranging from
$5. per hour or up to 33-1/3% of the funds recovered or secured.
The rate is highly dependent on the ability to pay and the inherent
value of the service to the client.

Many agencies and institutions are establishing positions for
ombudsmen within the framework of their organization. As an
independent or free-lancer you will be working through these people in many situations. You will also be developing the expertise
to act as a consultant in setting up ombudsmen programs in colleges and universities, hospitals, public schools, municipalities
and some progressive industries.

LOBBYING FOR LEGISLATED PROFITS

Industries and associations find it beneficial to attempt to influence legislation which affects their interest by a process called
lobbying. The person who maintains a personal contact with federal legislators and their offices to promote the passage of favorable laws and the elimination of unfavorable ones must be
registered as a lobbyist. Many states also require lobbyist registration. There are also varying disclosure requirements relative to

the lobbying budget and how it is spent. Some groups or industries prefer to call their lobbyists by other titles such as legislative liaison or government consultant or various other euphemisms. The registration requirement goes with the function, not the title.

Seth L. moved from his family's farm to his state's capital city in hopes of finding fame and fortune. A history major in college, Seth's lack of experience was a drawback in landing a job. Sitting in the visitors' gallery of the state legislature listening to a discussion of a bill affecting farm labor, Seth observed "Why, they don't understand what that bill is going to mean to folks back home." He wrote a letter to the farm cooperative group to which his family belonged advising them of the bill and asking authorization to speak for the group. He also asked for $2,500 in expenses "to tide me over while I work to defeat this bill."

Seth got the $2,500, registered as a lobbyist, and managed, with the help of other farm group representatives, to kill the bill. It was an exhilarating experience and one which inspired him to contact other groups whose interests were involved in legislative discussions. That was the beginning of one of the most prestigeous lobbying firms in the country today.

Lobbyists for major organizations are usually salaried, with compensation ranging upwards from $20,000 a year. Smaller organizations, or those whose needs are infrequent or periodic turn to lobbying firms which take clients on either a project or retainer basis and handle a number of interests at one time. Fees for a project, i.e. a special legislative concern, can be as low as $2,500 plus expenses. Annual retainers, which are negotiated in advance, generally start at $7,500 and go up depending on the prestige of the lobbyist and the financial ability of the client.

The lobbyist or government consultant is responsible for keeping the legislators informed on the issue at hand. He or she prepares and disseminates factual information justifying the legislative position being taken by the client. In some instances, the lobbyist will prepare legislation and find legislators to introduce it as well as other legislators to support it. Lobbyists will often write speeches and articles for legislators who support their interests. They will also attempt to secure time at committee and pubic hearings to promote their client's point of view and try to determine the way each legislator will vote on any particular bill, developing strategies to influence the negative or undecided voter.

While a great deal of the work of people like Seth is done in normal business hours, social contact with legislators or their aides on an informal basis is sometimes part of the job and often most effective. So, lobbyists are also party throwers and, hopefully, party goers. They also tend to congregate where they anticipate chance opportunities to discuss their clients' interest with those whose actions will affect them.

Many lobbyists have come from the ranks of government employees or politicians who have some knowledge of the legislative process. Political science majors and journalists who have had experience covering the government scene have also made their way into the ranks. On the other hand, people who have a strong familiarity with the objectives of an industry or an organization have, like Seth, also become lobbyists and learned their way around the states' and nation's capitals.

It is important to know that lobbying, within the framework of the law, is a perfectly respectable career and is engaged in by many people in a participatory democracy. While lobbyists represent special interests, these include not only "big business' but also consumer groups, welfare groups, rehabilitation, etc.

THE PROFITABLE BUSINESSES
FROM GOVERNMENT CREATED NEEDS

1. Establish a tax service to help individuals and small businesses fill in and file their income tax returns. If you don't have the background on your own, you can investigate franchised tax services.

2. Develop and sell record keeping systems to enable individuals and small businesses to more easily keep track of their taxable income and tax deductible expenses. Check-sized files or expandable divided file envelopes can be adapted for this purpose, using various colored labels to designate categories. Sell by classified ads and direct mail.

3. Sell laminating or framing services for government required posted licenses, notices and signs. Check phone

book yellow pages or salesmen's opportunity magazines for equipment sources and pricing suggestions. Find your market among those mandated to display such material. Use direct mail and trade journal advertising.

4. Investigate anti-pollution regulations and locate manufacturers whose products meet government requirements. Become a manufacturer's representative for as many non-competitive lines as possible. Sell to affected industries, municipalities, and housing development sponsors.

5. Establish an "instant printing" service to meet the need for rapid multiple copies of grant proposals, applications, and various forms. Lease photocopying, offset printing, collating and binding equipment direct from manufacturers who will train you; or investigate franchised services. Expand your income by serving small businesses and individuals on walk-in basis, but seek out regular clientele to form backbone of your business.

6. Develop testing laboratory and field testing services for testing water supplies and discharge waters for contaminants, required by law under the various pure waters and environmental control laws. Secure annual contracts for testing services from firms, housing developments, resorts, institutions and municipalities affected by the laws. The procedure is simple. It's just a matter of following accepted methods and developing a schedule and reporting system.

7. Take advantage of the bonanza business in personal and small business profit sharing trusts and pension fund programs now permitted as deferred taxable income. Become a representative for banks, insurance and investment firms eligible under the law to provide acceptable programs. Or provide a consulting service for individuals and small businesses to help them select the best program for their special needs. Or provide a special bookkeeping service to fill out the numerous forms required annually under the new laws and regulations.

8. Using information available from the government printing office (Superintendent of Documents, U.S.G.P.O., Washington, D.C.) and from other government agencies,

publish and sell informational leaflets on almost any subject, from calorie counts and food preparation to mandated standards and requirements for most industries. Most government printed material is in the public domain and can be reprinted without copyright infringement. When in doubt, check for authority to reprint.

9. Publish a newsletter for individuals, businesses and libraries, providing information on new special interest publications by government agencies and the government printing office. Or write a column for newspapers and trade magazines covering the same information.

10. Using resources of state and federal commerce departments and small business agencies, conduct a series of small business management seminars.

7

MULTIPLYING PROFITS
FILLING THE NEEDS
OF SINGLES

LILA'S SINGLES MINGLES

Widowed at 48, Lila E. had never worked a day in her life. Hers had been an early marriage to a successful salesman who had managed the family's money. Lila was distraught when she learned after he died that her financial reserves were limited. Typical of many women who had never earned a salary, she believed she had no real marketable skills.

The thought of applying for a job and getting turned down terrified Lila. Almost as awesome was the thought of landing the job and having to keep regular hours. The solution, Lila decided, was to find a business she could start on her own, one which required little or no investment and one which would fit the life-style to which she had become accustomed.

"As a widow," Lila notes, "I suddenly became aware of how many women there are who not only hadn't worked during the years of their marriage but also had not socialized without their husbands. Many women wanted to date men or at least to have male escorts for particular occasions, but opportunities for meeting seemed limited to embarrassing introductions from family and friends."

As Lila recognized this need, she took stock again of her own assets and interests. She had a nice home. She was a good hostess. She liked to have people around her and to help them, if possible.

From this assessment, Lila developed her Saturday night Singles Mingles and insured her future. Having first contacted her own widowed friends who assured her of their interest, Lila placed an ad in the personal column of her newspaper.

> Single men and women over 40 can meet others
> in comfortable home surroundings for conver-
> sation, cards, companionship, cake and coffee.
> Singles-mingles evenings, $5.00 per person.
> Send name, address, age and phone # to Box
> #SP.

When the answer came in — forty the first day — Lila phoned each person, secured personal references, and after checking them out invited 24 men and women to her home for the following Saturday night. "We wound up with more than 24," Lila recalls, "because some people were too insecure to come by themselves and asked if they could bring a friend. And some others who had said they were coming backed out at the last minute."

Lila averages 30 people at each of her Singles Mingles which are now held on Wednesday, Fridays, and Saturdays. She figures she clears around $200 a week. In addition to the expenses for refreshments, she pays one of her widowed friends to help with the hostessing chores, preparing name tags, and serving the refreshments.

ANALYZING THE NEEDS OF SINGLES

Lila created a successful business because she found a way to fill a particular need of a particular group of singles. But the singles market in this country is so vast and varied that there are hundreds of other opportunities for those who want a business of their own.

In analyzing the needs of singles, one must remember that there are various age groups — from eighteen to over eighty — various interests, and various cultural and attitudinal differences. The singles market includes not only widows and widowers and divorced men and women, but also the unmarried and unattached and the confirmed bachelors and spinsters. In a preponderance of cases, singles spend their money to fulfill their own needs rather than those of others. Except for the divorced with alimony obligations and those singles who are raising children, there is more money for non-necessities in the singles market than among most other groups in similar income brackets.

Some of the needs of singles are fairly universal. Singles invariably offer a good market for individually portioned foods and for cookbooks featuring recipes for one or two servings. Judging from the spectacular growth of singles' apartment complexes, singles' bars, and publications devoted to singles, there are many commonalities of interest which point to capital opportunities for the enterprising.

Generally singles have more leisure time to fill than their married sisters and brothers. There is consequently a need for activities to fill time. There is also a need to combat loneliness, to be with other people of similar interests and lifestyles, to find companionship and friendship, and, for some, to find someone with whom to share expenses and their lives.

The theater, cinema, opera, ballet, symphony and other cultural and entertainment events attract many singles, as do spectator and participation sports. Other singles turn to learning situations, lectures and courses, while still others involve themselves in crafts and hobbies, reading or travel. This list is not much different from the spare time pursuits of married people, but there are essential distinctions in the approach. These are:

1. As a rule singles are not comfortable with marrieds. They do not generally share the same viewpoints or problems and even if they do they feel like "fifth wheels."
2. Because their responsibilities to others are less involving, singles generally can be more flexible in their plans.
3. While many singles cherish their privacy, they are often uncomfortable going places alone.

Recognizing these distinctions can put you on the track of dozens of money making businesses.

CAPITALIZING ON THE NEED TO FILL TIME

Geoffrey F. started his cooking classes for single men as a once a week activity while he worked as an assistant housewares buyer in a department store. Today, his cooking school income almost equals his salary and Geof is giving up his job to devote more time to his own business.

Four nights a week, each for a different group of twelve single men, Geof conducts a class which prepares an entire meal. Students pay sixty dollars for a series of five once a week lessons. The fee covers their dinner each class night and is considered quite reasonable. Menus take advantage of weekly and seasonal specialties and of convenience-based recipes which can be completely prepared and ready to eat in 90 minutes or less. Classes start at 6:30 p.m. with dinner each night scheduled for 8.

"We deal almost completely with meals planned for two people, except for dishes which can be made in quantity and frozen in individual or two portion servings," Geof notes, "and we lean toward things that look difficult or exotic because they make a great impression."

Geof's recollection of how his classes began is worth recounting, since it illustrates a section of the singles scene.

"I used to see so many guys spending a half week's pay taking girls out to dinner and the girls weren't even impressed. I figured that any fellow could learn to create a spectacular dish or two and really impress a date, save money and incidentally eat better. My first students were friends and guys who worked with me at the store. They spread the word so that I had to keep adding courses and to keep a waiting list. Since I vary the menus seasonally some men have taken four courses."

"I suspect that a lot of them come back as much to have something to do as to learn how to cook. But, I really don't question why they come. The money is good. More than half the fee is profit."

Geof is now considering a deal to franchise his schools. His new condominium apartment, almost completed, will have a custom-designed kitchen suitable for 24 students.

"That will bring in a lot more money than my job and leave me time to work on the franchise deal and a cookbook," Geof says. "But first I'm taking a singles cruise. I wouldn't mind meeting a gal who wanted to run cooking classes for single women."

CLAUDE R. CASHES IN ON THE NEED
FOR TOGETHERNESS

Claude R. is a charming bachelor who drives a Silver Cloud Rolls and maintains luxurious apartments in four major cities. This might not be extraordinary were it not for the fact that Claude had neither a cent nor the scent of a job ten years ago when he became a singles promoter.

Claude recognized the need of singles to fill their leisure time along with their need to be with other singles. He also knew the needs of cruise lines and resorts all over the world to fill their soft calendar spots, as we discussed in Chapter 3. He learned to fill these by organizing singles cruises and resort vacation packages. Because he is willing to speculate and make a commitment for a block of rooms or cabins he negotiates a much lower than individual rate. He then establishes the rate at which he will sell the package, pricing it slightly under the individual rate charged by the shipping line or hotel, but high enough to be profitable for himself. Depending on the potential demand from his singles lists, he can tack on a profit of from 7 to 10%, considerably more than the 5% group commission he would receive if he did not "buy" the rooms in advance.

Claude also serves as a consultant to resorts, on annual retainers ranging from $2,500 to $7,500 a year. This income and the status it has given Claude is a direct result of his recognition that the successful singles program must create a social structure in which it is acceptable and easy to strike up a conversation. To earn his retainers, Claude develops schedules of ice-breaking activities, games, tournaments, lessons and parties which literally require people to talk to each other. You can cash in as Claude has. The singles market is vast and worldwide in scope. You can develop a singles list in your own bailiwick and promote it for international tours or for nearby trips. Cruises to nowhere which cover a long weekend have become popular singles vacations. Of course, you can go along free if you negotiate this extra with the shipping line or resort. It's wise, to protect your interests, to have negotiated rates, package extras if any, and commission arrangements secured in writing.

Because some singles group promoters have not always fulfilled their obligations either to the singles they've served or to the hotels and cruise lines, you can expect any proposal you make to be carefully scrutinized. Nevertheless, because the profit potential is constant and worth working for, it is well worth perservering.

If you are interested in becoming what is popularly called a "singles promoter," the procedure is simple though it may be time consuming. Before you start, it would be worthwhile to attend a few singles parties organized by others.

The first step is to compile a current list of singles for whom you can play the role of Pied Piper. Some lists are for sale through direct mail firms or list companies. Other lists can be purchased from or traded with other single promoters. Sometimes it's possible to get lists of members from clubs which are predominantly or entirely singles or by checking the residents of single's complexes. You can also develop your own lists over a period of time by running dances and or parties for singles.

DOLLARS FROM DANCES

If you run singles dances your clientele will come chiefly from word of mouth and from advertising. Many newspapers run their singles' promotion ads in a separate classified section on Thursdays to cover events scheduled for Fridays and Saturdays. Singles dances or parties are a lucrative business in areas where there is a sufficient singles population. To determine the number of singles in any area, check the area Chamber of Commerce or Commerce Department office or write to the U.S. Census Bureau for demographic information for your area.

The singles party or dance involves 1) renting a space to hold it; 2) providing a band or canned music (tapes and records); 3) developing a format for introducing people and getting them to mingle; 4) seeing to it that refreshments are available either included in the admission fee or to be purchased; 5) attempting to secure a balance of male and female guests and a compatible age range.

Depending on the area, the place and the type of refreshments, you can charge from $5.00 up per person. You have to play your first few events close to the vest, anticipating a minimum attendance and setting your rates by at least doubling your costs. It is preferable to select a room in which the anticipated crowd will appear comfortably crowded rather than one so large the group seems small. It's a good idea to have folding screens, large plants, or other decorative items handy to make a large room feel smaller if necessary. You can promote to separate age groups, i.e. over 26 to 30, or you can advertise without specifying. It's good insurance to invite a few singles as your guests to keep the party moving and to spread the word to their friends. In addition to advertising in the papers, you can post notices at community centers, singles' bars and apartment complexes, in area delicatessens or supermarkets in which singles shop, and in office buildings.

If you are successful in attracting a following you can expand your activities to include group tours, vacations and cruises, theater parties, dinners, mystery outings and other activities to meet the interests of your group and attract newcomers. The procedure is to estimate the number of people you believe you can get to participate. Using this, or a range, say 40 to 50 or 100 to 125, check with the group sales department of the resort, cruise line, theater, etc., and make the best deal you can for commission or rates. In the latter case, add on your estimated promotional costs and expenses and your profit margin. If a guarantee or a deposit is required, make sure that you have the leeway of a cutoff date on which to finalize numbers or cancel out without penalty. You can usually make such an arrangement if you are promoting for dates which are ordinarily slow periods. After you've developed an attractive package and the rates, you have to promote to your following and if necessary to others. It is important that you secure deposits with reservations. Otherwise you will find that people who have signed up frequently change their mind at the last minute. If, for any reason, you find you cannot develop enough interest for a successful and profitable event, cancel before the cut-off date and return the deposits. If you are booking a group into a singles cruise or resort program where others are also booking and the establishment is also taking individual reservations, you can get by with a smaller group than if you are planning a separate program of your own.

TEDDY D'S MYSTERY MONEY

Teddy D. earns $15,000 or more each year running a Mystery Mingle Club in his spare time.

"You don't have to write a who-dunnit to make money with mysteries," Teddy says, "but it helps to have a great imagination and a nose for discovering out-of-the-way places and experiences."

If you organize a mystery mingles club for singles (or for couples) you will collect an annual membership fee ranging from $12 to $25 This will entitle members to one or two mysterious destination parties and the opportunity of attending a mystery event each month at a "greatly reduced" fee. Memberships are secured by direct mail and advertising as well as by offering free renewals to members who bring in a quota of new members. The mystery is provided by not telling members in advance where they are going for the mingle. You either invite them to assemble at a particular public place at a fixed time and transport them en masse to a destination, or you give them the address to which they should go for a surprise event. Clever clues can be given in the invitation, and some people may guess correctly, but the objective is to provide programs which people don't ordinarily develop or attend by themselves. A further objective is to diversify the experiences so that you hit a responsive chord for each person at some point throughout the year.

Some of the programs you can arrange for are: group attendance at an introductory lecture given by a self awareness organization like "EST" or Students International Meditation Society (Transcendental Meditation); an evening with a stage hypnotist or a fortune teller; a tour of a newspaper or publishing plant or a nearby manufacturing facility; a visit to a winery or a visit from a wine producer's representative, with samples; a private screening of an old classic film; a boat ride, a visit to a greenhouse or farm; a lesson at a specialty or ethnic cooking school or at a famous restaurant; a tour of city hall or the state capitol; a lecture by an astrologer or an E.S.P. or astral projection disciple; a visit to a craftsman's or artist's workshop; a tour of manufacturers' outlets, etc.

Some of these programs will cost you little or nothing to arrange. Others will have a fixed charge and still others will have a per person charge. If you are providing transportation you will have costs for renting or chartering limosines, autos, jitneys, buses, horse and carriages or what have you. You will, of course, have your fixed costs for advertising, printing, mailing, phone, insurance, etc. If your membership gets very large, you may need to pay others to share your role as host or hostess or tour guide. You may also run into some expenses in planning each program or in making a trial run before you take a group out and, possibly, tips along the way.

If you control your costs carefully, you can nearly always double them and often go even higher and still provide a good buy for an afternoon or evening of companionship with an interesting or off-beat experience. It is wise to assess the spending potential level of your membership either in conversation or by questionnaire to determine the average charge most members would pay. If you use this technique you can select programs and events which fit into that category and still provide an adequate profit for you.

Teddy advises that the key to discovering places to go is careful research. Chambers of Commerce and tourist information offices are good sources. Most states put out guide books which can be secured from the state department of commerce. Many newspapers and magazines periodically list things to do in the immediate area. Feature articles which you might clip and file often cover interesting places. Colleges, universities, museums and galleries offer advance calendars of events. Off-beat magazines or special interest publications provide other sources. Once you start making contacts, you will find that people begin giving you ideas. Suggestions will also come from your membership. While it all sounds like fun — and it is — it's important to remember that it is a business and requires serious control of income and expenses.

MINING THE GOLD IN SELF IMPROVEMENT

While many singles spend a good part of their income on entertainment, vacations, tours and other indulgences, many others feel the need to develop new interests, talents, skills, and, not incidentally, new contacts with other people.

The success of Geoffrey F's cooking classes for men is just one example of thousands throughout the country. If you have any expertise in anything at all, you can cash in on the craze for classes, courses, and workshops especially among the single set.

Junior colleges, community colleges, and universities are continually on the lookout for people to develop and teach non-credit courses in their adult or continuing education programs. Usually the institution will sponsor a course whenever 12 or more people can be anticipated to enroll. Sponsorship includes providing a place, on or off campus, publicizing and advertising, and, of course, paying the instructor. Payment is by the hour, by the number of students enrolled, or by a formula which takes both factors into account. Subject matter can be almost anything from needlework and crafts to survival training. The paraphysical interests seem to be well received. Indoor gardening is another popular subject and can be broken into several popular courses such as "gardening under lights," "flowering plants and how to grow them," "greenhousing," etc. Other popular courses include memory improvement; folk, square, and ballroom dancing; ethnic history and literature; political action; nature study, conservation and preservation; film making, broadcasting, and play production; yoga, karate, and physical fitness, etc.

While most non-credit courses are taught in the evening, there is a growing trend toward day time scheduling for singles who work odd or off hours, retired folks, and senior citizens. There is also a trend toward Saturday sessions for children.

To develop a free-lance teaching schedule, first prepare a proposal. This should include a brief overview of the course or courses you are offering, a tentative course outline, any costs involved for equipment or supplies, and the time frame. Courses may run for one, two or three hours, once or twice a week for eight to twelve weeks. With the proposal you should be prepared to discuss the potential class enrollment, your own interest in the field, and your ability, if any, to recruit students through personal contact or otherwise. When you are satisfied that you can present your ideas enthusiastically and well, contact the director of the continuing ed program by phone or by letter to request an appointment.

If the thought of a college or university turns you off, you can teach in your own home, a rented store, loft, or barn, or a community center or church.

BUILDING A CLASSY BUSINESS

You can supplement your income from classes with a complimentary supply sales and service business. Or, you can reverse the procedure, beginning selling supplies and teaching classes as a means of promoting business. This is particularly profitable in the field of arts, crafts and hobbies. Eva S. spent $250 on a pottery kiln and arranged for a consignment supply of clay and molds, greenware (unfired pottery), bisque (fired but not glazed), and glazes. She started out at home with a class of 18 who paid her $3 an evening for her informal classes, purchased their supplies from her, and paid a standard fee for use of her molds and for having their work fired. As her classes expanded to three nights a week, she converted a room to a display and sales area and added potter's wheels, kilns, and allied supplies for ceramic hobbyists. Eva's sales business now has become her major money maker while the classes continue to bring in new customers and pay the expenses of the operation and sales help. That $250 original investment has grown to nearly $5,000 in inventory and supplies, but Eva is not complaining. She's been clearing $18,000 a year from her classes and clay.

The same technique can be used to develop a business with plants or needlecraft or woodcrafting or any other craft or hobby. It should be remembered, however, that the interest in various crafts is cyclical. There are many enterprising people who are ready to capitalize on the newest enthusiasm. The ones who succeed are those who have researched the market thoroughly; established a business-like control of expenses and income; and are flexible enough to add new products and services as old ones slow down in profit potential.

SERVICING THE NEEDS OF SINGLES

We've discussed the needs for companionship, entertainment and self-improvement. Dating services, marriage brokers, escort bureaus, travel clubs, house parties and classes of all types can be profitable answers to these needs. There are innumerable other needs to be filled.

In a Midwestern college town, two college students rented a house and advertised it as "your address as far as your parents are concerned." Growing numbers of collegians, it seems, are living with roommates they'd rather not have their parents know about. Now, for a fee, they can use the house address as their own. For an additional fee, they can move into the house if their parents visit. A mail and message service with 24 hour phone answering service is also provided.

The business is too new to know how profitable it will be for its originators, but it demonstrates how needs create opportunities.

LUXURIES FROM LIVE-ALONERS

"I've never really researched it," Nadine R. says, "but I'd bet that most pet owners are singles. At least they seem to spend the most money on their animals."

Nadine's elegant boutique for pets, called Pups-Purrie, earns a fancy living for her and the craftspeople who supply her wares. Nadine started the shop with her own silk screened pet birth announcements and birthday cards. She also sells custom painted needlepoint likenesses and pet portraits done in water color, sepia, and oils, with prices ranging from $50 to $250 depending on the size and medium.

"Starting this way," Nadine remarks, "I didn't have to invest much money in inventory. I had about $300 tied up in my cards and portrait samples. All I really had to worry about was the rent, $300 a month, and the utilities which averaged another $100 or so. But as my business developed and I had extra cash, I put it into exclusive items — one of a kind doggie sweaters, coats and blankets, handcrafted leashes, identification tags and traveling baskets, feeding dishes, placemats and toys. I take a 100% markup on most items and find a ready market. For many hand-mades, people place holiday orders months in advance. It gets so busy during December that I close for a month after Christmas to spend some of my loot. Last year, my third in business, I cleared $22,000."

Many live-alones are a good market for pets and for the services and supplies pet owners need. Singles in particular need someone to walk, water and feed their pets during vacations, holidays or sick days. Dog training and grooming services are well patronized in heavy singles areas. There is also a need for pet transportation to and from veterinarians and kennels.

Brian G. earns over $200 a week as a pet photographer. "It takes a lot more patience than photographing people, but it's a satisfying business," Brian advises. Brian specializes in photographing show dogs and breeding stock, advertising in pet journals as well as by direct mail to lists of show entrant owners. Incidentally, the technique can be applied to photographing horses as well. A bit of research will show you the proper stance of horses about to be photographed. There are a number of excellent markets within this category. Included are racing horses, pet riding horses, show horses, etc.

SPECIAL NEEDS OF P.W.P.'S

Parents without partners have special needs. Seminars for single parents have profit potentials as do workshops and lectures for the recently divorced. The need here is for ego building or self awareness.

The need for child care is often a basic prerequisite if the single parent is to work or enjoy any social life. Housekeeping and child sitting services or registries might be considered to fill some of these needs. Playschools in your own home can attract children of singles as well as those of two working parents. Tutoring services for youngsters are frequently in demand by single parents, fearful that they are not meeting their full responsibilities.

MULTIPLY $ FILLING SINGLE P.N.S

1. Start a singles newsletter. Offset or mimeograph. Advertise free subscriptions, but charge $5 for listing of name, pseudonym, phone or box number and special interests. Be prepared to forward box number replies. Capitalize on the lists you build up by selling to a singles promoter.

2. Invest approximately $1500 in sound equipment and popular records and offer a "disco" service to bars, restaurants and private parties. Charge from $75 to $150 depending on what a live band goes for in your area (the disco service should be less).

3. Remember that singles often become doubles, officially. Establish a wedding consultantship, handling everything from clothes, invitations, favors, wedding feasts or parties, flowers, and honeymoons. Either establish a commission from vendors or a percentage of budget (15% is fair) from your clients.

4. Specialize in a particular aspect of weddings. Learn how to make fabulous fabric floral pieces, decorations and bouquets. Sell to department stores, wedding caterers, churches, gift shops, or directly to engaged girls.

5. To meet the need for having the proverbial button sewn on and other minor clothing repairs, you might open a mending service in your own home or apartment. Establish a minimum fee of $2.00 per garment.

6. Cater to the need to know what's going on where. Publish a free monthly calendar of happenings in which singles might be interested. Sell advertising space to singles bars, apartment complexes, and single promoters

at $25 per column inch per issue. Distribute to newsstands in high singles areas.

7. Offer a course in financial management to recently divorced men and women. Alimony cuts into many males' money know-how, which many pre-lib women never had an opportunity to learn. Charge $18 for a one evening 3 hour course in basic budgeting, banking and saving principles. Up the price for investment counseling. Or charge $35 for a three session, 2 hour a week, program.

8. Organize a shopping combine club for singles, buying specialty foods in small or individual size portions, cans, or jars by case lots or other less costly multiples. Charge $25 annual membership fee, $1.00 service charge per order, additional for home delivery. Deal directly with wholesalers, distributors and restaurant suppliers. The club may not save singles money, but it will save waste, foster better eating, and provide a meeting place and conversation piece.

9. Create an "Everything Registry." Sign up people who will plant, pet-or-child sit, pick up, deliver, cook, clean, repair, cater, etc., for a fee. Add on 20% when you refer them to temporary employers. Advertise in pennysavers.

10. Cater to the need for "A Taste Of Home." Cater ethnic meals for lonesome loners. Develop a repertoire of Greek, Italian, Jewish, Lebanese, German, Indian and other foreign-origin home cooked specialties. Advertise in pennysavers, area Anglo-ethnic publications, and on shopping center notice boards.

8

CAPITALIZING ON THE NEED TO FILL LEISURE TIME

ANALYZING THE LEISURE TIME MARKET

Future industrial planners tell us that in the not-too-distant future the average work week will be less than thirty hours. When that comes to pass, the average wage earner will have more free time than time on the job. Now, if you don't think that's going to create tremendous needs, ask any housewife whose husband just retired.

Some wit once said "the future is a moving target." In reality, the future is now. At least the needs to fill leisure time exist today in vast and varied markets; and there are still opportunities to get in on the ground floor and ride your "elevator" up to the plushest penthouse you can picture.

Claude L. discovered his "elevator" in singles cruises and resort vacations. But there are millions of singles who wouldn't be caught dead in that milieu — and they offer millions of dollars in opportunities. Senior citizens — and more people are living longer — are another moneyed market for leisure time spending.

These two groups form the obvious market. The less obvious markets, however, are no less lucrative. Take housewives whose children have left home. Or, take teenagers. With fewer job opportunities open to teenagers, they are at leisure during school holidays and summer vacations. If their families are also free at these times they become part of a family market. If not, they represent huge amounts of money on their own, even if it's not coming out of their own pockets.

Penny C. who needed to pay off a $10,000 education loan, exploited this market with her unusual travel camps for teens. "While there are still successful summer camps, lots of sophisticated teenagers and even pre-teens refuse the regimentation and the sameness year after year," Penny explains. "There are also teen tours of varying types. But my program combines group travel with camping experience. That is, we organize our tours for sightseeing or entertainment values, but we spend our nights at camp grounds, cooking out and sleeping in tents. We travel in a chartered bus with 48 youngsters, 12 to a counselor. Four of the older youngsters are counselors-in-training who come along at half-fees and each is assigned to a group. Before each season, I scout out the route, make camp ground reservations, arrangements for group sightseeing and special programs, and place orders for meats, groceries, fruits and vegetables. Our fee has been $200 a week, per four week session. I ran two tours a summer, averaging about 25% profit, around $20,000. It's hard work, a 24 hour day responsibility for those eight weeks, but its more money than most people make in a year, and it didn't require much of an investment."

While some sophisticated teenagers might scoff at traditional summer camps, specialty camps are still attracting their fill. Tennis camps, all-round sports camps, music and drama camps and most recently, reducing camps, have become great money makers. Under normal circumstances the investment required to buy or build such a facility puts it out of reach for most of us. The rising costs of energy and taxes, however, has made it possible in some areas to lease at very reasonable fees old estates, hotels, motels and even private residential schools. Area bankers as well as real estate agents should be contacted to determine the availability of such low cost rentals. State and local regulations relating to camp facilities should be thoroughly checked. If a suitable property can be leased, and you can show a banker a sheaf of signed reservation forms and deposits you may be able to borrow sufficient operating capital to see you through till the balance of campers' fees are paid. The key to profits in a camp is the percentage of occupancy. The "nut" or basic costs remain approximately the same if you have 200 or 250 campers. Once you've covered the "nut" the percentage of profit per camper increases enormously.

It's quite possible, even probable, that summer camps, generally considered children's facilities today, will become family facilities in the future as growing numbers of older people have more leisure time to fill.

LEE C. FILLS HIS COFFERS FILLING OTHER FOLKS' TIME

Lee C. had a job as a bank clerk but "it wasn't going anywhere and didn't provide the income I wanted for my family. I knew I had to come up with something better. But when that something came up, I almost missed it."

Lee's mother-in-law had married young, raised a large family, and now "had nothing to do." Lee suggested a job but she insisted "I've never been trained for anything special. What can I do?"

Lee contacted the state employment service and arranged for "Mom" to take some aptitude tests. The result confirmed what he knew about his mother-in-law. She was great with people, painstakingly neat and accurate, and had an aptitude for secretarial skills. He convinced her to take a part-time job as a dentist's receptionist and to take an evening course in typing.

"You know, "Lee grins from behind his expansive glass topped desk "it wasn't until she said it that it hit me. What she said was, 'You could make a fortune as an employment counselor.'"

Lee's not making a fortune — yet — but he's making $40 an hour in his own counseling office advising, for the most part, middle-aged women how to fill their leisure time profitably and ` rewardingly.

People who are interested in people, who are articulate and inventive, and who can investigate career and educational requirements can enter this type of counseling on a full or part-time basis. Beyond being credible, there are few, if any, formal requirements for the counseling position. While some states require certification or licensing for psychologists, most do not have fixed criteria for employment or educational counselors. Do check your own state requirements before you hang out your shingle.

HELPING PEOPLE DEVELOP PROFITABLE HOBBIES

The need to fill leisure time is not mutually exclusive of the need to earn additional money. Indeed, many people seek to use their free time to earn extra cash. You can develop a profitable business helping them develop their potential.

Joey Y. teaches classes in magic. He charges $25 for a series of five one-hour lessons and averages a dozen students to a class. The students are predominently retired men who go on to earn $25 to $50 a performance at private parties, clubs and organization programs and at conventions. Joey maintains a registry for those who wish to be booked through his efforts, charging the usual agent's ten percent. In addition, he takes orders for magician's supplies and tricks of the trade which he picks up from a wholesaler as necessary.

Simon Z. teaches would-be stage hypnotists. His fees are higher, $75 for 6 lessons, and he offers no registry service. But people come from over 100 miles away and often go on to take an advanced course as well.

Sheryl C. offers lessons in puppet and marionette construction, at $50 for four two-hour sessions, and an additional $25 fee for a three-hour workshop on play production for puppet and marionette theater.

Cynthia L. runs a catering service and "school for caterers." She charges $60 for four three-hour sessions. She offers courses in appetizers, buffet dishes, salads, desserts, and bar-tending; and serves as a registry for her graduates. Cynthia's income, over

$20,000 from classes, catering and registry, is augmented by selling professional chef's supplies, disposable party supplies and unusual serving dishes.

Madeline C. teaches needlepoint for nothing to people who buy her custom-designed kits for chair coverings, pillow faces, frameables, and personal accessories. Kits sell for $7.50 for an eyeglass case to over $100 for a custom designed portrait. Madeline will take orders for finished needlepoint usually at 3 times the kit price, and farms these out to willing students.

The list of profitable hobbies you can teach is limited only by your own interest. The market for new skills is large and growing. The investment in most instances is small, the rewards gratifying. In many instances teaching part-time, several evenings a week or on weekends can bring in as much income as a full time job. It's always wise to start teaching on a part-time basis, expanding your schedule as it becomes profitable to do so.

PROFITS IN SIMPLE PLEASURES

Thelma and Steve H. hadn't planned on a family until their furniture, stereo and color T.V. were paid for from both their earnings as nurse's aide and orderly on the seven to three shift at the city hospital. But they still owed $700 when Thelma became pregnant. After several weeks of worrying and serious thought, Steve decided that he could never send his son to college on his salary alone.

Looking for a business they could start on a borrowed shoestring, they hit on the idea of The Read Around, to cater to the needs of the stay-at-home leisure timer. Steve borrowed $500 from the hospital employees' credit union, rented a small store near the hospital and bought a half dozen tables at the Salvation Army. For $50 he bought all the paperback books they had there and at every other thrift shop in town. They put a notice on the hospital employees' bulletin board and spent $3 for an ad in the area pennysaver to explain the way the Read Around worked. They offered to buy selected used soft-cover books for up to 1/4 of their initial price and to sell them at half their original price tags. They also advertised a trade of any book of equal value for a 25¢ fee per trade. Initially, Steve switched his shift to the 3 to 11 P.M. so he could open the shop at 10 each morning, while Thelma came in from 3 to 8 P.M., when she closed it.

Read Around cleared $40 the first day.

After a very short time they were able to pay off $200 on their installment loans and to invest $50 in shelving. By the time Thelma had to give up her job at the hospital, the store was bringing in nearly twice her salary and they were able to hire part-time help. Steve continued working at his job for another year. Then they opened Read Around II, and Steve became a full time businessman with an income approaching $22,000.

While catering to the need to read was profitable for Thelma and Steve, opening up the great outdoors opened a bank account for Doug and Lisa R. They conducted weekly nature walks in nearby parks Saturday and Sunday at 10 and 2. The walks, lasting about two hours each, covered a three-mile trail along which Doug and Lisa identified trees, shrubs, and wild plants describing their medicinal or nutritional values. At $2.50 a person, the walks brought in close to $100 a day during good weather.

To meet the need for bad weather outings, Doug and Lisa made arrangements for "indoor tours," nature films rented through a school supply catalog and shown in a senior citizen center whose residents saw the films free in return for use of the hall.

WERNER L'S SECRET INGREDIENT

Werner L. started a travel agency in a busy shopping center and after a year couldn't earn enough to pay the rent. When he discussed the problem with his bank loan office, he said, "I don't know what's wrong. I keep recommending the best buys in vacations. I keep up with all the bargain packages, but my clients don't come back."

"Maybe you're downgrading your clients," the banker suggested. "Even though nobody wants to spend more than is necessary, this clientele may want to go first class all the way. They might want to be pampered and feel special. That's why they come to you instead of booking reservations on their own."

Werner went back to the agency and called a cruise office. "I'd like to plan a first class escorted cruise for 25 couples," he said. "What can you do for me?"

Werner advertised his "escorted cruise" package with home to ship limosine pickup and return, a champagne bon voyage party to which clients could each invite a guest, a cocktail party tendered by the agency one night out, and a captain's cocktail party during the week. In addition he advertised "an experienced traveler will accompany the group to assure you of first class treatment all the way."

An invitation to join the cruise was sent to 500 area professional people, and a poster went up on the agency window. The 25 cabins were booked within a week. Werner and his wife accompanied the group and saw that each client was properly cared for.

"The escorted tour turned the tide for me," Werner says. "I learned that for lots of people first class is the only way to travel. The high ticket vacations pay higher commissions of course. That doesn't hurt, but the best money comes from repeat business and recommendations. The secret ingredient for success is personal attention, making people feel extra special. When you come down to it, we all have that need and we don't mind paying for something that satisfies it."

TEN WAYS TO ADD LUXURY TO YOUR LIFE
FILLING LEISURE TIME NEEDS

1. Establish a used sporting goods shop and exchange for skates, skis, tennis rackets, camping equipment, tents, etc. Accept goods on consignment and take 33-1/3% of the selling price; or buy outright at no more than 1/3 of original retail. Pay less if you're buying at the end of the season and have to tie up your capital. Avoid buying anything you can't reasonably double your money on. Make extra bucks repairing equipment, sharpening skates, waxing skis, restringing rackets, and mending tents. Unless you start with a hoard of your own or can get enough consignments, plan on $1,500-$2,000 for initial inventory.

2. Become a sports "pro." Give private lessons in swimming, ($5 per hour); tennis ($10 per hour plus court costs if any); skiing $10 per hour), or give group lessons at $3 to $5 per person. If you can, use public facilities. Or contract with a private facility to provide free group lessons for their guests for the privilege of selling private

individual lessons on your own. Investigate the possibility of running a "pro shop" on a commission basis.

3. Create a "What's Doing Where" guide for your area covering all cultural, sporting, recreational and special attractions. Get your area Chamber of Commerce, merchant's association or tourist commission to purchase enough copies or buy enough space to underwrite printing costs. Sell advertising space to food establishments, motels, hotels, theatres, etc. Distribute free.

4. Contract for fresh produce booths at flea markets, fairs, sporting events. Sell seasonal produce, purchased either at wholesale markets or from the farmer. Apples, peaches, watermelon slices are best sellers for in hand eating. Sell produce by the piece, bag or basket to avoid weighing hassles. Check need for permits and licenses.

5. Open a bonded house-checking service for vacationers at a $10 per hour fee. Offer to check heating and plumbing facilities, pick up mail and newspapers, water plants and lawns, feed pets, etc. Check insurance company for bonding.

6. Give young mothers some leisure time daily by establishing a play school for tots in a spare room, heated garage or basement. You can handle up to a dozen preschoolers by yourself; charge from $15 to $20 per child for a 3 hour session five days a week. Invest a few hundred dollars in sturdy toys, games, a record player, etc.

7. Organize a sporting goods rental registry. People with campers, snowmobiles, canoes, sailboats, skis, surfboards, etc., pay you $2 to have their item registered for rental when they're not using it at a fee which they establish. You add on 10% to each fee. Advertise in classifieds and pennysavers.

8. Invest $300 to $500 in commercial barbecuing equipment, steamers, etc. and become a caterer for chicken and steak barbecues, clam bakes, corn feasts and other mass feeding menus for summer fund raisers, fairs and large private parties. Your own truck is handy, but you can get by with a rental. You'll require help for large groups. Easiest way to charge is a guaranteed minimum of $100 above costs (they pay food supply bills direct)

and 50¢ per head for everybody over the first 200. Earn additional money by renting concessions at fairs, flea markets, etc.

9. Open a public game room in a loft or store. Invest in games — checkers, chess, backgammon, cards (no gambling), Monopoly and other board games. Charge $1 admission and $1 an hour. Make extra money from vending machines for snacks and soft drinks.

10. Save flight or cruise bound vacationers hassle, time and even money by driving them *in their own cars* to and from the airport or docks. Charge $5 an hour plus out-of-pocket expenses for tolls, gasoline, meals on the road, etc.

9

BUILDING UP CREDITS IN FOREIGN EXCHANGE

SPANISH DOODLES TO DOLLARS

If it weren't for a church school scholarship, Rosita A. couldn't have attended the American college she did. Even on the scholarship the going was rough. Her family in Mexico was poorer than poor and she longed to be able to help them. Her campus job in the dining hall was hardly enough to take care of her own expenses let alone to send gifts home.

It was when she went to buy a birthday card that she discovered the need which has made her a businesswoman. There simply were no Spanish language cards. In fact there were no foreign language cards at all. Back in her room, Rosita drew some line drawings reminiscent of home and added a birthday verse in her native tongue. The first one went to her father. The second one was used for reproduction with a hand cut silk screen. She made a hundred copies and hand-folded and glued accompanying envelopes. With an enclosed note, "Hand screened cards by Rosita, $3.00 a dozen to retail at 50¢ each," and an order blank, she mailed the samples to college book stores and to famous department stores in cities where she knew there was a Spanish speaking population. That mailing brought orders for ten dozen and a request, "Can you make some Christmas cards and birth announcements which we can sell in packs of 10? We'd take 100 packs of each at $2 a pack."

Rosita could. They did. Today Rosita's parents and three younger brothers work the silk screens, and the packing and shipping department of her American plant while she travels to Mexico and other countries to develop new ideas for her foreign language greeting card lines.

THE NEED FOR FOREIGN LANGUAGE SKILLS

The concept of American society as a melting pot caused many immigrants to learn to speak English and deprecate their native tongues. Today there is more of an acceptance of ethnic differences, a growing respect for those who can communicate fluently in more than one language, and a serious need for their services.

The need to communicate is, of course, so basic that we hardly think about it except when we can't. Standing in an elevator, for example, when everyone is speaking a language we can't understand is a frustrating experience. Imagine the anguish of a foreign speaking parent if a child is injured or ill in a hospital, or if there is a misunderstanding in school or the law. Consider the difficulties of business contacts and contracts between people whose languages and customs are different. Think of the marvelous tastes and textures of an ethnic experience that might be enjoyed by other groups.

"Imaginate" the markets for foreign exchange and you'll bank lots of good American dollars.

A MIX OF MARKETS FOR THE FOREIGN TOUCH

1. The ethnic market for ethnic products and services
2. The ethnic market for American products and services

3. The American market for ethnic products
4. The foreign market for American overseas
5. The American market for Americans overseas
6. The foreign market in America

THE ETHNIC MARKETS

Rosita capitalized on the ethnic market with her foreign language greeting cards. Marco sold his services as an ombudsman chiefly to ethnic compatriots in his neighborhood. Among the needs of an ethnic community (which may be spread over the entire country) are:

1. Traditional and Familiar Foods
    in groceries and eating places
2. Traditional Religious or Cultural Events
    and the necessary costumes, decorations, symbols and music
3. Common Language Media
    newspapers, magazines, books, radio and television

Jay S. won fame and fortune as a band leader, a field where many try and few succeed, by specializing in polka music for the Polish community in which he grew up. Today Jay's recordings are popular in the ethnic community throughout the country and he has won many non-Polish converts to the polka.

The ethnic cultures in America have enriched the country and brought wealth to many immigrants and their children. Chinese-American Jimmy L. is one of them.

MAKING CHOW MEIN MAIN STREET FARE

Way before Doyle Dane Bernbach created the "You Don't Have to be Jewish to Like Levy's Rye Bread" ad, Jimmy L. recognized the American market for his Chinese food. Jimmy's first job was washing dishes in a steak restaurant in a small mountain town. When the restaurant went bankrupt, Jimmy was desolate.

He wanted that restaurant so much he could taste it. He had three hundred dollars in the bank from his nine months of dishwashing. When he heard that the bank held the installment notes on the bankrupt restaurant's equipment, he pleaded with the bank president.

"Lend me enough to stay open for six months," he said, and I'll salvage your notes and my loan. Americans like Chinese food. It's cheap, fresh, and I can make a good profit on it."

Jimmy got his line of credit with the bank and did just what he had promised. After a year, he made a down payment on the building. Today, he's one of the wealthiest property owners in town and owns a large share of bank stock as well.

MORE CASH FLOW WITH FOREIGN FLAVOR

You don't have to open a restaurant to earn money with ethnic foods. You can profit by preparing a specialty and selling it to restaurants or delicatessens. Greek moussaka or Italian lasagne, stuffed shells, meat balls or sauces, Israeli falafel, Jewish gefilte fish, Scandinavian herring salad, Mexican refried beans and taco sauce are just a few profitable items.

Or, you can simply make your recipes earn more dollars than you believe possible.

ROLLING IN RECIPE DOLLARS

Kathy R. lost her job and was facing eviction from her apartment when she remembered her Russian grandmother's recipe for stuffed cabbage. She borrowed two dollars from a friend, placed an ad in the daily paper:

> Russian Heirloom Recipe for the best stuffed
> cabbage you ever ate. $1. Katrinka, Box

Three days later Kathy went to the newspaper office and picked up 21 envelopes — each containing $1. She renewed the ad for 3 days. A week later Kathy had her rent money and a new career.

"If there's that much money in one recipe," she thought, "how about a whole Russian cookbook?" It took her a few days to test her recipes for "Blintzes and Borscht," a package of 24 authentic Russian recipes handwritten on 3 x 5 cards. This time when she placed her newspaper ad, the editor interviewed her. The ensuing orders at $3.50 each convinced Kathy that she had a promising business potential. She had her cards photo-offset and began advertising in out of area publications with similar results. Last year she made $7,200 selling individual recipes and cooking card sets by mail.

The American market for foreign flavor extends to clothing and furnishings as well as food. There's money to be made importing these items for direct sale to the mail order market, or to boutiques. You can investigate import potential from any foreign country by contacting its trade information service, usually attached to its consulate. You'll be provided with names of American importers with whom you can deal as well as with lists of contractors or manufacturers overseas. Importing however, requires a capital investment and is not without risks. As a beginner you might do better to deal with an established importer until you are thoroughly familiar with the business and market potential and have some risk capital to invest.

MARIA ELENA'S CATALOGUE OF CATALOGUES

Maria Elena De La Iglesia proved that you don't have to be an importer to make money from foreign goods. What she did was to contact major department stores and specialty shops throughout the world and request their catalogues for products they would mail or shop here. Then she listed by product the international sources of catalogues for distinctive products and good buys. To make this effort profitable, Maria Elena presented her idea and manuscript to a prominent publisher who bought it and pays her a royalty on every copy sold. *The Catalogue of Catalogues,* copyrighted by Maria Elena De La Iglesia, and published by Random House, is a guide to world-wide shopping by mail.

While catalogue shopping fills a need for some people, others will pay to have a personal shopper. That opens up an opportunity to cruise the cashways in foreign waters.

SHOPPING TRIPS CAN PAY YOUR WAY

You can pay for your trip abroad and buy some luxuries for yourself by taking orders for particular products before you leave and having them mailed or shipped directly to the purchaser who will pay the customs taxes, if any. If you're going to be handling lots of other people's money, you may find it easier to get assignments if you're bonded. You may also want to speak to your **banker** about the best ways to handle the money.

Advertise in the personal columns describing your itinerary and offering to shop or handle any other business for a fee. You won't make much on personal shopping (10 to 15 percent on what you pay is fair as long as you can't find the imported product already selling in this country for close to that) but even that will help get you there and back.

You can make more money shopping for business opportunities for others. A similar ad in trade journals or business columns can often bring in several profitable assignments. $100 a day is a reasonable fee to start with. Up the amount if you'll be handling extensive or valuable negotiations. For the most part the people who will contact you will offer a fee and it will be up to you to accept or reject it. It's wise to be wary of excessive sounding fees and to investigate such offers cautiously and carefully.

Americans who travel on their own can also carry money bags for you if you're going to be overseas for any length of time. They'll pay you more than a native guide to guide them and take them on shopping trips to the stores where natives buy as well as to the famed specialty shops. Advertise in major American papers before you leave and periodically while you're there, or promote your services to the tourist abroad.

HOW TO REACH THE AMERICAN MARKET ABROAD

Most major cities of the world offer some English language papers, journals, or magazines. (If there's none in your city and there is an English speaking market, there's a need you can fill.) You can advertise in these, or you can save money by posting cards on bulletin boards where Americans tend to congregate or visit: the American embassy or consulate, hotels, American Express, branch offices of American banks and sometimes at schools and universities.

While you're posting your cards, check the others on the bulletin boards for people *offering* opportunities to you.

AMERICAN IS A FOREIGN LANGUAGE

As soon as you get overseas you've added another saleable commodity to your personal assets. You'll find a huge market nearly everywhere for "learning to speak American." Parents will pay you to spend time conversing in English with their children; people planning to travel here are anxious for tutors; and foreign businesses frequently schedule classes for employees who are to deal with American businesses. You won't generally make much money by American standards — rates vary from country to country — but you'll earn more than the average native, and you'll make some interesting, even valuable, contacts you couldn't make in any other way.

HANNAH'S HOME AWAY FROM HOME

Hannah K. found another way to fill a need for Americans overseas and it enabled her to stay where she wanted to be.

She had come as a young bride to the Carribean island where her husband worked for a shipping company. When he died, she had become so attached to her home, the climate and the countryside, that she could not leave. But though there was a company pension it was not very much. Employment opportunities for American women were few, and Hannah felt she had few skills. As the Americans on the island and nearby areas came to pay condolence calls and Hannah received other such visits from American friends on cruises, she recognized that there was a need for them to be together periodically, to share news from home, to be insiders rather than foreigners.

To meet this need and her own, Hannah instituted her Sunday morning brunches for Americans on the island and American visitors. The thirty or so guests she serves each Sunday each pay $5, netting her close to $100 weekly.

WAYS TO FILL THE NEEDS OF FOREIGNERS IN AMERICA

1. Open your home to a foreign family. Most foreign countries have pensions, farm houses and even palaces where vacationers are welcome to stay — for a fee — and get to know how natives really live. In the U.S.A. the tourist

home, which filled similar needs, has almost become extinct. But it's profitable, not too difficult, and worth looking into not only for the not-so-occasional foreigner from overseas, but for any visitors to your area. If you have an extra room or rooms, *make* them work for you. Even if you charge dollars less than area motels you'll profit because you have to pay your overhead anyway.

2. Act as an interpreter for foreign businessmen. Advise consulates, embassies, trade centers, airlines, hotels and universities and research facilities of your availability. Average rate for an interpreter is $5 per hour.

3. Translate technical or scientific papers for research centers, medical schools, business and industry. Average rate for such translation is $12.50 per hour, or for a negotiated fee, by the page.

4. Serve American businessmen by conducting private tours for foreign businessmen visiting firms here. Charge firms $10 per hour per person plus out of pocket expenses, entertainment and admissions costs. Use company cars if possible; if not check your auto insurance and necessary permits or licenses for your own.

5. Become an ethnic marketing consultant for commercial hotels and resorts, banks, investment companies and industry. Advise on advertising themes and media, public relations and promotional programs, multi-language signs, staff training programs, adaptions to customs and culture. Fees run from a minimum of $40 an hour to over $1,000 a day.

6. Serve as a translator for law enforcement agencies and courts in the interrogation of foreign speaking victims, suspects and witnesses. Fee averages $12.50 an hour.

7. Develop a business meeting the needs of pharmaceutical companies, hospitals, doctors and other health care practitioners for multi-language information for the laymen. New laws requiring "informed consent" and the malpractice insurance crisis have increased the need for information directed to the patient in *language he can understand*. It's a new field and you can fill it with posters, pamphlets, signs, letters, records, audio visuals, etc.

8. Become a shopping consultant for foreign visitors. Prepare a list of good department stores, designer and specialty shops, American craft boutiques and art galleries in your area. Advise foreigners where to find what they're looking for; accompany them as interpreter and adviser. Set your fee at $75 per day, or 10% of their purchases, whichever is higher.

9. Become a free-lance foreign language copywriter for advertising firms serving multi-national clients. Fees run $10-$25 an hour, or are paid on a negotiated price per assignment.

10. Establish a registry of foreign speaking men and women available for any of the above assignments and for baby sitting and governess jobs as well. Advertise your registry to hotels, airlines, business firms, etc. Farm out assignments and collect 10-15% of the fees.

10

RICHES AND REWARDS FILLING NEEDS OF WORTHY CAUSES

AFFAIRS THAT PAY OFF FOR PEGGY

Peggy V. has held affairs in schools, churches, hotels, motels, ballparks, meadows, planes, trains and boats. But her reputation improves with age and her last child will soon finish graduate school on the money she has earned.

Peg runs fund raising events for political candidates and charitable organizations. She is, in her own words, "a dedicated promoter." She'll undertake to plan and coordinate all of the fund-raising events of a three month campaign for $300 a week plus expenses. With organizations, she works either on a per week fee or a percentage of gross proceeds from 10% to 25% depending on the price of admission — the higher percentage from lower priced events.

"I'm not a fund raiser," she says, "but my promotions raise funds and that's what I sell. If I'm going to run a $200 a person dinner, I may have it served informally around a chuck wagon in a meadow — under tents, of course, God forbid, it should rain, — or wrapped in red bandanas on the end of hobo sticks, or served around the swimming pool of the richest member of the club. I look for pizazz and profits. The first attracts people to the events. The last keeps clients calling on me. Sometimes, though, an event is so much fun, we repeat it every year and it becomes a tradition."

Peggy can run several functions for several charitable organizations at one time by staggering the final dates and the lead time. "I have one secretary steady and hire additional people in my office when necessary, billing the client for them. Every organization committee usually comes up with enough dedicated volunteers to do the leg work and the real selling. I develop the idea, direct the operation and make sure things get done. That takes one day a week or less for the first four weeks, one to two for the next three, and three days generally for the week of the event. Dates should be scheduled and announced as early as possible and the organization members can be working or making ready, but 8 to 12 weeks give plenty of lead time for a good response.

Peggy's clients come to her by referral from her political contacts. "But," she points out, "there's a lot of business out there — Junior Leagues, hospital auxiliaries, religious organizations, private schools, children's charities, just about every nonprofit group around needs money to fulfill its objectives. There's lots of ways of raising money, too. All kinds of benefit performances, circuses, ball games, operas, plays, brunches, lunches, dinners, midnite suppers, even breakfasts, casino cruises, and hundreds of others."

You can succeed in this type of business by bringing to it a creative imagination, good organizational abilities, serious attention to details and deadlines, a peck of patience and a bushel of charm to encourage volunteers, and some good common sense. With these attributes, you can learn almost everything you need to know working as a volunteer in a professionally run event or reading about such events. What you can't learn that way, you have to learn by experiences. Every fund raiser has some lulus!

YOUR OWN TIME FOR MONEY MAKING

In the trade Peggy is a promoter in the field of sustaining fund raising. John R, whose work we discussed in Chapter 4, specializes in capital fund raising. The distinction between raising money for buildings and new projects *or capital fund raising* and raising money to keep the projects going or *sustaining fund raising* is important. People tend to give in proportion to the goal in capital fund raising, with some gifts running into the millions of dollars. While some annual or sustaining fund campaigns are run in a somewhat similar goal oriented fashion, most raise money through a series of events or ongoing projects rather than through direct solicitation of funds.

The more prosperous organizations often have staff people to handle fund raising programs. The smaller or less affluent groups hire free-lancers. Both generally turn to outsiders for capital campaigns and special promotions. You can take on the projects which interest you, when they interest you, working 52 weeks a year or any number you choose. You can work on your own or build an organization of "account executives" who will handle clients under your supervision. It's up to you. You can get richer than you are, filling the coffers of worthy causes.

ROGER'S FREE SALESPEOPLE SAVED HIS LIFE

Roger D. had, through no fault of his own, lost three jobs in a year. A fire took one, an urban renewal program knocked out another, and the owner's death finished the last one. With no prospects in sight, he reluctantly turned to unemployment insurance, growing more and more depressed as the weeks rolled by.

Hoping to borrow some money to meet his car payments, Roger went to see his friend Tom Z. He found Tom making small wooden toys.

"I've been selling them at flea markets for three bucks apiece," Tom said, "but the market around here is pretty well saturated and I don't know how to get rid of them."

Roger took a bunch of samples. "Let me show them to some buyers in the city and see whether I can sell them."

He made the rounds of all the major stores.

"Wrong time of year," said one buyer. "Too high priced for us," was the turn-down from another. "A church bazaar item," remarked the third.

On top of everything else, this failure seemed like the last straw. Roger D. was literally beside himself. He called his friend Tom to tell him the bad news, the thought crossing his mind to say good-bye forever, then suddenly he put down the receiver and walked — no, ran — to the nearest church rectory.

Roger left his samples with the pastor's wife — on consignment at $2.00 each for the church bazaar. The store buyer proved correct. The samples were sold out early and 43 orders were taken. The Mother's Club decided to handle them as a regular fund raiser.

Today Roger and his friend Tom are in partnership producing toys. They don't have to sell them one by one. A great army of fund-raisers in groups across the country save them the effort. Roger promotes sales to groups by direct mail. "We cleared $11,000 each last year" he grins. "Those women are great sales-ladies."

INVENTORIES MAKE THE WHIRL GO ROUND

One of the first things a fund raiser learns is that most organization doers and givers thrive on recognition. There are few who prefer anonymity. Though most people protest the need for rewards, you've never seen resentments smolder till you've seen a chairman or chairlady overlooked when thank-yous are passed out.

Awareness of the need for recognition opens the door to filling that need with promotions, devices, and incentives. The classic incentive in capital fund raising is a touch of immortality, the enshrinement of a donor's name on a building or a room in the building. But that's not what we're talking about here. We're concerned with the day to day devices that bring repeat orders.

You can represent firms selling pins and emblems or those selling bronze plaques. You can represent a number of firms with non-conflicting lines. Or you can go into business for yourself.

Jess B. did after a heart condition forced him to retire from his job driving a city bus. He invested $2,500 in used photographic equipment, some precut sheets of aluminum, a transfer lettering kit and some mounting boards. Working in the den of his apartment, Jess recouped his original investment within three months. He got his first big order because he understood the need for recognition. This is how he sold it.

A hospital was in the midst of a three million dollar building campaign. Each day the city paper carried a story about someone who had been named to head some fund raising committee or sub-committee. Roger secured a black and white photo of the architect's rendering of the building. With his lettering kit he printed beneath the photo:

> This building could not have been built without the dedicated and devoted efforts of John G.

He prepared the plaque (in a process you can learn in a few hours). Then he took the completed plaque to the campaign chairman who immediately noted that John G. was just one of the sub-committee chairman. "If we acknowledge one, we have to acknowledge them all," he said. "Can you give us a special price for 24? They'll be a good incentive for our chairpeople to bring in their quotas."

Since he could use the same screen just by changing the name of the recipient, Jess set a lower per plaque price and came out with an order for nearly $1,000.

"If I had realized what was going to happen I might have given those plaques away for nothing," says Jess. "I can trace almost all of my local customers back to those plaques."

LET YOUR CLIENTS DO THE TALKING

Jess discovered another important facet of doing business with non-profit organizations. We discussed in previous chapters the fact that aggressive executives often become involved with worthy causes to improve their own business image or their chances for moving ahead, while wealthy men and women serve in such organizations to fill their special needs. As a result, the officers and boards of most community groups usually represent a cross-section of leaders in many spheres of influence. More than that, they generally are active in more than one organization and they

are communicators. They may not take your product door to
door, but their casual comments open doors you might never
have been able to unlock.

As a result of his hospital order, Jess now makes all the retirement plaques for a major area plant, the annual officers'
plaques for three service clubs, and all the plaques the school
athletic department requires.

These steady orders are bread and butter business. The orders
that flesh out the meal are from individuals. With his equipment
Jess makes plaques from diplomas, professional licenses, portraits,
birth announcements, wedding invitations and even newspaper
and magazine pages.

"I have a yellow page listing for people who let their fingers do
the walking," Jess says, "but most of my business comes when my
customers do the talking."

YOU CAN SELL TO THE FUND RAISING MARKET

Girl Scouts sell cookies. Boy Scouts sell light bulbs. High school
seniors sell magazines. Nearly every group is selling something.
You might think the market is saturated. That's not so. We'll
discuss the answer to this seeming paradox in a few minutes. First,
to help you "imaginate" some opportunities, let's examine the
fruits you can pick from the fund raising money tree.

Five Fruitful Approaches to Fund Raising Needs.

1. Products for fund raisers to resell at a profit.
   Examples: Roger's wooden toys; fruitcakes; cookies;
   candies; light bulbs; greeting cards; flower bulbs; jewelry; etc., handmade or commercial.

2. Programs and projects and promotions to raise sustaining funds.
   Examples: Peggy's special events; (Also see Chapter 4,
   Playing at Hard Work); Development grants (See Chapter 6); Fund raising journals; direct mail appeals; auctions; cookbooks; marathons; telethons; etc.

3. Services to keep organizations going.
   Examples: Rubin Kranur's mailing service, (Chapter 1);

John R's capital fund raising (Chapter 4); Jonathan L's comprehensive association service, (Chapter 5); newsletters, annual reports, speech writing, photography, conventions, etc.

4. Services to keep organizations growing.

   Examples: Jess B's incentive and appreciation plaques; Prize incentive programs; public relations; advertising; membership campaign packages, etc.

5. "How To Do Its" For Organizations.

   Examples: Books; pamphlets; newsletters; seminars; audio-visuals; conferences; training programs; etc. to show a group how to do any of the above.

HOW TO SELL TO THE FUND RAISING MARKET

We said this market is wide open even though there are many people already profiting from it. The reason is that fund raising thrives on new approaches. A housewife can use only so many potholders, or whatever it is a group has been selling. Events that become "old hat" tend to fall off in income. Volunteers need the stimulus of creative new approaches.

These needs often make it easier to break into organization business than into the commercial market place. In addition, the market is well defined. You can secure lists of church and synagogue affiliated groups, hospitals and their auxiliaries, service clubs, fraternal orders, youth groups and many others. You can make this a really big business.

Abe Wolf recently took a trip around the world after retiring from a silk screen business which produced printed neckerchiefs for scout troops.

Mrs. W. turned her small house into a fruitcake factory and moved her family to an expensive ranch with the profits from tons of cakes she sells to fund raisers.

What you need is a product with special appeal to the special market, i.e., neckerchiefs for scouts, or one which has wide appeal to the middle class market. Edibles are perfect because they're consumable. That's why so many groups sell fruitcakes, candies, nuts, cookies, and preserves. It does not have to be hand-

or-homemade but there must be a reliable source for a uniform product at a stable price.

With some exceptions, the best fund raising items sell in the $1.49 to $2.98 retail category. You should be able to sell to your groups for between 1/2 and 2/3 of the suggested selling price and still make at least a 33-1/3% profit on costs. For example: if your costs are $.75, you sell for $1.00 and the group sells for $1.49; if your costs are $1.50 you sell for $2.00 and the group sells for $2.98. You can set your prices in this fashion for orders of a dozen or more items ordered at one time. You can charge more if fewer are ordered. Firms vary in their approach to shipping and handling charges. Some include them in their costs so they are reflected in their prices to groups. Some charge extra for shipping. Others absorb shipping charges on orders over a certain minimum.

You have to watch your markets carefully. Some items are continuous sellers, bringing repeat orders, year after year. Some saturate a particular market quickly. Don't despair. You can sell other groups in other areas or you can add new products. Or you can do both — cautiously, testing the new waters one toe at a time.

TEN WAYS TO PROFIT FROM THE FUND RAISING MARKET

1. You can help organizations present beautiful certificates, scrolls, and personalized awards if you become a *calligrapher,* a hand lettering specialist. You can learn from books available in your library or craft shop. Your original investment is lots of practice time and a little cash — about $25 — for materials. Your average charge of 5¢ a letter or 50¢ per name adds up quickly with group orders. Charge more for work that involves two or more colors, special layout, etc.

2. Annual report preparations are often farmed out by many hospitals and other organizations. Your fee for developing the format, photography and writing, selecting type, and arranging for production can average $150 a day or $1,500 for the approximately 70 hours you'll need to get the average job to the printing stage.

3. Organize an annual trade show for fund raisers at an

area school, armory or hotel. Sell booth space to individuals and firms who sell — or want to sell — to the organization market. Invite members of all nearby fund raising organizations to attend free or at minimum charge. Booth space goes for $50 to $250. Start at the lower rate if you can't estimate first year response. Increase rates as organization members attendance goes up. Promote event early and consistently to sell booths and increase attendance.

4. Become an identification tag specialist. Sell name tags, booster buttons, badges and other paraphernalia for meetings and conventions. Start by representing a variety of non-conflicting suppliers. Gradually acquire your own equipment.

5. A free-lance writer on a capital fund raising team earns $300 a day plus expenses — which can include hotel bills, meals and travel. You'll write brochures, news releases and speeches. Check with capital fund raising firms for opportunities.

6. Provide a child-sitting service for organizations which want mothers of young children to attend their fund raisers. Charge $1 per child per hour. Most places where such an event is held have a room which can be used for this service at no extra cost.

7. Offer a complete service for fund raising journals. Develop format with an area printer; page rates with organization committee. You prepare the solicitation literature, direct the volunteer solicitors or hire a team of phone solicitors to sell journal space. You handle copy, layout, etc. Your fee can average 20% of the gross income. Project requires three months lead time but not necessarily full time all through.

8. Collect examples of successful fund raising ideas used all over the country and publish a monthly fund raising exchange newsletter. Charge $30 to $50 a year.

9. Become a group sales representative for a hotel or motel. Develop lists of convention and fund raising chairpeople and solicit them for convention groups, fund raising vacations and incentive reward vacations. Your fee is 5%.

10. Help small as well as large club treasurers comply with
    federal and state regulations for financial reporting by
    nonprofit organizations. You can set a minimum $25
    fee for setting up a bookkeeping procedure which will
    produce the necessary reporting information quickly;
    or you can develop and market a kit with instructions
    an record keeping books. Charge at least 3 times your
    cost for kit.

11

HOW TO FILL A HELPING HAND WITH PROFITS

THE PLEASURE OF RONALD'S COMPANY

Fifteen year old Ronald M. was big for his age, but hardly seemed big enough to carry the responsibilities of four younger brothers when his mother lost her job. He was afraid his brothers would join the street gangs who were intimidating the neighborhood with purse snatchings and muggings. Even his mother was afraid to go out alone.

That's when Ronald started his business. Every day after school and on Saturdays he escorted groups of women and older men to the neighborhood markets and various other destinations along the way. He charged 50¢ per person. "I wasn't fussy about the time," he says. "It usually took about an hour and fifteen minutes. It got to be a social occasion for the older people.

They'd lived in the neighborhood for years, but most of their friends had moved or died and they didn't know most of the new people. Some of them would give me tips and make presents for me. They'd come out even when they didn't need to buy anything. In the summer, sometimes they asked me to stay with them in the park so they'd feel safe. Sometimes we'd have two or three trips a day. I averaged about a dozen people each trip. If there were many more, one of my kid brothers picked up the rear."

"We wound up with fifty, maybe sixty dollars a week. It kept us going till Ma got her secretarial job back and it helped me through college."

Ronald expects to earn his degree in sociology this year. "I'd like to work for an agency that would help those kids in my neighborhood," he says. "They sure do need help."

THE HELPING HAND MARKETS

If recent trends continue, health care will become the biggest industry in the country. All around us, even today, people are making fortunes meeting the needs of this market. Not just doctors and professionals, but also lots of men and women with no special skills but the ability to see a need and the good sense to fill it.

To analyze the health care market and "imaginate" its opportunities, it should be separated into direct and indirect categories. Among those included in the direct health care market are:

1. People in reasonably good health seeking preventive care
2. People who don't want to have children and those who want to but can't
3. Pregnant women
4. The sick and the injured
5. The physically, emotionally or mentally handicapped
6. The infirm or senile

The indirect health care market consists of people, agencies and institutions which cater to the needs of the direct market. Among these are:

1. Physicians, dentists and other health care specialists; nurses, technicians, therapists, etc.
2. Public and private agencies and organizations
3. Hospitals, nursing homes and other primarily in-patient facilities
4. Medical, nursing and other health related educational and research facilities
5. Druggists and the pharmaceutical and medical supply industry
6. Clinics and ambulatory care centers
7. Unorthodox alternatives
8. Professional and lay communication media

There are opportunities in both the direct and indirect markets. Janice C. earns over $700 a month taking orders for nurses' uniforms and shoes. Clare E., clears nearly $15,000 a year as a free lance medical illustrator. Manny B. has parlayed a $3,000 investment in care into nearly a million dollars worth of assets in seven years.

MANNY'S RESIDENTIAL CARE

When a 12 bed private hospital was forced to close because it did not meet new government standards, Manny B. investigated to see whether it could be approved as a residential facility for senior citizens. The standards for the residential care facilities are less stringent than those for health care institutions. Some states do not have standards or licensing procedures for residential facilities at all.

Manny was able to buy the hospital with $3,000 of his own money and a mortgage from the former owners. He contacted the social service agencies in the surrounding area advising them that he would handle old people who could no longer take care of themselves, but who did not require hospital or nursing care. The need for this type of facility is acute in many places, and most residential care homes have lengthy waiting lists. Some times these facilities are called senior hotels. Rates run from about $600 to several thousand dollars per month, depending on how plush the facilities are. Manny's home was filled almost immediately. While some oldsters came by themselves, many were referred by social service agencies which in some instances paid the fees through welfare programs.

He hired a middle-aged couple to cook and keep up the building and grounds. A cleaning woman comes in every other day to clean the public spaces and help the residents with their rooms. Manny himself comes in for an hour or two every day after he leaves his full-time job. He handles the business end, ordering supplies, paying bills and record keeping.

He made $17,800 the first year. "Not a fortune, but enough so that I was offered a $30,000 profit if I'd sell. I decided to keep it even though I knew the profits wouldn't go up very much."

After two years, with nearly $40,000 in profits, Manny began looking for another larger facility he could buy inexpensively. He found and bought an old 30 room hotel for $75,000 about fifty miles away.

Most recently, he acquired an 80 bed building for nearly $200,000. "My properties are going up in value," Manny says, "not only because I bought them at good prices, but because I have made them useful and profitable business properties. If I sell them now, I don't sell real estate alone, I sell a going business and that's worth a lot."

If you are interested in getting into residential care for senior citizens you should check for all governmental regulations which might affect you. Federal and state welfare programs, building codes, licensing standards, etc., are changing rapidly in this field. In many instances local or county welfare agencies may be able to direct you to sources of the necessary information.

UP TO $1,000 A MONTH IN YOUR OWN HOME

You do not have to run a commercial facility to lend a helping hand and a home to the helpless. You can earn both love and money by becoming a foster parent. Children are placed in acceptable homes, generally for limited periods of time, by many religious or social service agencies.

In addition you may help house mentally retarded children and adults who would otherwise have to be institutionalized because they have no homes. Despite their disabilities, those who are placed can attend to their own physical needs and are able to work at ordinary tasks. If you are sensitive to these peoples' needs and can provide a warm and secure home for them, most states will pay you to do so. Rates are about $250 per month for room and board. Clothing and medical allowances are generally provided. Generally no more than four at a time are placed with any one family.

For information check with your local or state mental health agency, association for retarded children or social service agencies.

HELPING PEOPLE STAY AT HOME

Every sign points to home health care as the millionaire-making industry of the future. The costs of institutional care in hospitals and nursing homes have been driven to near-crisis points. Inflation, more adequate salaries for staff and increased sophistication of medical equipment and services all contribute to the spiraling costs. Government reimbursement programs such as Medicare and Medicaid and insurance plans such as Blue Cross, Blue Shield or other commercial health and hospital insurance programs have a huge stake in reducing the costs of health care. So do unions and companies whose fringe benefits include payments for hospitalization.

A study by the U.S. Department of Health, Education and Welfare indicates that 33⅓% of patients in nursing homes could receive adequate care at home. A U.S. Government Accounting Office report concludes that a quarter of all patients are treated in facilities beyond their needs.

Currently, these people go to hospitals and nursing homes instead of being cared for at home for two reasons. Adequate home care professionals are not available or organized to serve their needs; and adequate reimbursements are not generally provided to stimulate such organizations or to make it advantageous financially for the patient to stay at home.

The Council of Home Health Agencies points out an instance in which a man recovering from a stroke received 17 weeks of intensive home care including 50 visits by nurses, therapists, a speech pathologist and occupational therapist. The cost was $1230. In a hospital the cost for 17 weeks would have been nearly ten times the amount or $11,900.

Some agencies and insurance plans are already reimbursing to some extent for some home care services. Additionally such organizations as the American Cancer Society, the Arthritis Foundation and the Multiple Sclerosis Association provide some funds for home care.

In most areas where home care services are available to any extent they are being provided through community health agencies. In those communities where commercial organizations have established home care services, they have been eminently successful. The home care industry will grow at a phenomenal pace when reimbursement agencies and health insurance plans reimburse for home services as they do now for hospital services. No one who doesn't have to be in a hospital really wants to be there.

You can get in on the ground floor of this helping hand industry by establishing a home health care team registry. This would include homemakers and health care aides, nurses, physical and occupational therapists, laboratory and diagnostic technicians, and other professionals who would be available on a freelance basis to handle the physician-prescribed treatment to the patient at home. You can secure professionals for your registry by advertising and publicity and also by posting notices at hospitals, health educational facilities and in professional association newsletters or bulletins.

You can secure clients by notifying physicians, social service offices, hospital discharge planning offices, and voluntary health agencies.

You can make money for yourself by receiving a 10 to 15% referral fee from the professionals you assign to clients. In this instance professionals would set their rates including your fee. They would be paid by the client or the reimbursement agency or insurance plan.

You could also create your own company of health care professionals, or arrange to employ them yourself and assign them as needed. This type of business, effectively managed, can make more money and lends itself to a franchise operation. It involves however, considerably more financial and management skill and a larger investment of time, effort and money.

$50,000 A YEAR AND A SHARE OF THE SAVINGS

Morris H. had a job as a bookkeeper and a wife who couldn't make ends meet on his salary of $9,800 a year. He began to develop headaches and a nervous stomach. He hated to go to bed because he tossed and turned until he finally fell asleep — and then he had nightmares. Afraid of losing his job, he finally went to see a doctor for some tranquilizers.

As he went through the examination, he said, "Listen, I know I'm not sick yet, but these money problems are driving me out of my mind. If I could earn half the money you make I'd be healthy as a horse."

"Being a doctor today is no cinch, either," the doctor replied. "We're snowed under by paper work in the office and the hospital. There are dozens of forms to fill out for each patient. The secretaries and nurses are never satisfied and I have no patience with them. I try to take a day a week off to be with my family and there's always an emergency. My desk is full of bills I haven't got time to look over. I like being a doctor, but I hate business."

"You need a business manager," Morris said jokingly.

"Would you take the job?" the doctor asked seriously. "One of the girls is leaving."

Two weeks later, Morris began work at a salary of $11,000. First he tackled the billing procedure for private pay patients, Medicare, Medicaid and insurance companies. Then he reorganized the office staffing. Next he got into the accounts payable for office and medical supplies. That led him to comparison shopping.

The doctor's accountant could not believe the improvement he saw in the businesslike operation. "You're wasting your time working for a salary. You ought to ask for half of what you've saved. Maybe you ought to become a consultant for other doctors. Most of them have no patience with business."

Today Morris and his wife have no money worries. He handles

five medical groups as a consultant, spending one day a week with each. He's organized a buying group for his clients to save them money over and beyond his office efficiencies. His income is over $50,000 a year and he sleeps like a baby.

Business managers for physicians and medical groups are beginning at salaries ranging from $15,000 to $75,000 a year, depending on the size of the group and the volume of business. In some instances the business manager becomes a member of the professional corporation and shares in the profits. Newspaper ads and professional agencies provide leads to such jobs. Or, like Morris, ask a friendly doctor.

GROWING MONEY THE NATURAL WAY

Wes and Sara J. cleared $3,600 last year from carob candy balls they made on Friday evenings and sold to health food stores on Saturday.

A college student, Gerry H. averaged $14 a day making 80 to 100 vegetarian sandwiches (sprouts, avocado, lettuce and onion; grated raw vegetables and cashew cream; baked eggplant and cheese; etc.) which he sold to near-campus restaurants.

Lynn S. started with a 79¢ pot of chives from her local supermarket and now earns $150 to $200 weekly selling fresh and dried herbs to health food stores and at flea markets and craft shows.

Sherry K's yoga classes, three nights a week and twice on Saturdays, attract 10 to 12 people at $3 for each 90 minute class.

A two day course in reflexology (finger pressure massage) goes for approximately $100 a person and attracts 30 to 100 people at each session.

All of these people are making money in the alternative health-care, self-care, field. The field covers hundreds of specialties from acupuncture and bio-feedback through vitamins and Zen. It is another field whose potential has barely been scratched. You can begin your investigation of the market by studying the publications generally available in a health food or natural vitamin shop.

You can take a healthy profit from this market in countless ways if you keep an open mind about alternatives to orthodox health care and combine your enthusiasm with sound business practice.

TEN PROFIT MAKERS FOR THE HELPING HAND MARKET

1. Equip a van with a ramp or lift for wheel chairs. Transport the wheelchair bound to doctors, schools, ball games, etc. Charge twice the average taxi fare for your area. Check licensing, permits and insurance.

2. Establish a rental service for home-care equipment (hospital beds, wheel chairs, crutches, bed pans, bedside commodes, etc.) Watch want-to-sell classifieds to pick up inventory, buy government surplus or contact hospitals which are modernizing.

3. Help people learn where to go for help with health and welfare problems. Compile a booklet listing all of the individuals, agencies, associations and institutions which offer such help in your area. Sell booklets (mimeographed or photo-offset) for $3 each by mail order, or for $2 through fund raising organizations.

4. Organize a vegetarian pen-pal club. Charge $5 a year for membership and three names and addresses. Advertise in alternative health, natural food, and vegetarian publications.

5. Create a business-service business for yourself and opportunities for the physically handicapped. Establish them as sub-contractors for work you contract for such as legal and manuscript typing, telephone calling or polling, small goods assembly, envelope stuffing and addressing, etc.

6. Develop "Executive Fitness Programs" for area industrial firms. Charge $50 to $100 a firm weekly for 3 one hour exercise regimes for their desk-bound executives. Require physician approval for beginners. Follow regimes which start slowly and increase gradually.

7. People who can't or won't lose weight on one diet or program are always ready to try another and misery loves company. You can compete successfully with nationally advertised reducing plans with a well balanced 1,000 calorie a day diet, a physician's scale, and a weekly meeting place. Charge $3 per meeting and pour on the encouragement, reducing recipes and understanding.

8. Invest $200 or less in a good quality juicer and sell fresh vegetable and fruit juices at flea markets and fairs.

You'll need a cooler for your supply of ice cubes, fresh vegetables and fruits (carrots are usually the base); a source of electricity; and paper cups. Make up snappy names for combinations you concoct.

9. Organize investment and office management seminars for doctors, dentists. Put together a team including an accountant, lawyer, pension plan advisor, etc. Charge from $75 to $175 per person per day exclusive of hotel and meals. Promote at least 3 months in advance with scheduling for major cities of the country.

10. Establish a prescription pick up and delivery service for one or several pharmacies in your area. Charge 10% less than taxi fares. In many instances it will pay a pharmacy to pay you rather than to own a vehicle and employ a driver.

12

GLEANING GOLD FROM THE GOLDEN YEARS

FORTUNES FROM THE FOUNTAIN OF YOUTH

Jean Paul S. once struggled to pay his bills as a small town barber. Today, the Frenchman who came to this country to seek his fortune winters in Palm Springs and summers on a yacht. His secret? Natural looking hairpieces for wealthy but aging men.

Lorraine T. turned her hobby, making cosmetics from natural substances, into a full time business earning over $10,000 a year. She developed an avocado and cucumber lotion to "help old skins look young again" and she tapped the Fountain of Youth. While some societies create a reverence for the aged, the American culture emphasizes the dynamism and the fresh look of youth. Because of this emphasis hundreds of millions of dollars are spent every year in this country for products and services to help people feel or look younger.

You can help people seek the Fountain of Youth and you can uncover treasures along their routes. You can enjoy the lush bounty of this growing market even if you're not a plastic surgeon who charges thousands for wrinkle-banishing face lifts.

The products and services you can sell to this market fall into several categories. Among them are:

1. Cosmetic products

   Examples: lotions, creams, bath oils, face masks, shampoos, hair colorings, make-up, wigs, hairpieces, hair-removers, etc.

2. Self-help products

   Examples: Exercisers, body-builders, diet programs, slimming apparel, saunas, steam baths, vitamins, herbs, health foods, etc.

3. Personal services

   Examples: massage, reflexology, cosmetology (make-up, facials, skin treatments, etc.), hair care, electrolysis, counseling, etc.

4. How-to-products and services

   Examples: lessons, classes, courses and seminars (or all aspects of self-care and beautification) given live or through cassettes, records, books, pamphlets, magazines, newsletters, visuals, etc.

5. Residential services

   Examples: health farms, beauty spas, rejuvenation clinics, etc.

LIFE LOVERS DROP LUXURIES AT DANA'S DOOR

Dana and Charles S. dabbled in every self-awareness and improvement program on the American scene, little dreaming that they'd literally land in luxury's lap. But that's what happened when they heard a doctor lecture on fasting.

The physician pointed out that many fasting authorities claimed it could relieve some health problems and add years to people's lives.

Dana bought a book on fasting. Then another. She became familiar with all of the authorities in the field. She learned how to start a water fast or a juice diet, how to come off one, and what to expect during the experience. She spoke to dozens of people who believed fasting had benefited them; and she recognized a real need.

Though fasting is perfectly safe if its done properly, most people are afraid to try it on their own, or if they do, find too many distractions at home to keep it up," Dana states. "People need a place where they feel they can fast under controlled conditions in a supportive environment."

With very limited capital, Dana and Charles began the search for such a place. They contacted real estate brokers within a 150 mile radius of the city, looking for a small year-round hotel that could be leased with a purchase option. They located a country inn property with seven small buildings and a total guest capacity of 140. It was owned by a childless widower who wanted to travel. The price was $280,000. But it could be rented for $3,000 a month plus utilities, maintenance and insurance. Charlie estimated it would take $18,000 to get by for the first three months and allow some money for advertising and promotion.

He would have preferred to start smaller. Dana, however, was captivated and determined to find a way to own it. "Give us 30 days," she asked, "to raise the money we need." The broker agreed. There were no other buyers in sight, anyway.

In the city, Dana and Charles invested $65 in classified ads and $35 for 2500 post card sized fliers, offering a controlled environment for fasting, juice diets and raw food regimes at charming Life Lovers Lodge. Rates were listed as $30 per week day, $75 per 2 night weekend, $200 per week, per person, double occupancy (25% surcharge for single occupancy). Those interested were asked to call for further information.

The flyers were posted in vitamin and health food shops; health clubs; meeting places for awareness, exercise and self improvement groups; recreation rooms of senior citizen apartment complexes; and at various spots in neighborhoods where they believed there were considerable numbers of European ethnics who might have been exposed to this type of spa in their homelands. Flyers were mailed to all the authorities who had written books and articles on fasting and to the slick high-fashion and beauty magazines.

"Charlie was still working," Dana recalls. "I sat by the phone and prayed, visualized, conceptualized, meditated and thought positively. Then the phone began to ring. There were a lot of curious callers. But that first day we got a couple and a single who wanted to make two week reservations."

"We asked for a $25 deposit per person which we agreed would be refunded if things didn't work out for them or for us. In the next two weeks we got 68 deposits and a lot of promises of reservations over a three month period."

"With about ten days left to that first 30 days, we had $2,000 in deposits. We called the broker and asked him to introduce us to the local banker. We told the bank what we had in mind, showed him the deposits and explained that they represented $11,000 in income — if we could get started. He offered us a line of credit up to $1,500. We borrowed $1,000 on the spot and paid the first month's rent. Our first guests came in two weeks later. We were able to buy the place — with a big mortgage — in 9 months."

Dana and Charlie are careful to make no promises of benefits or cures, nor do they prescribe any specific regime for any client. "We are not doctors and have no license to prescribe or treat," Charlie says. "We offer fasting, juice and raw food regimes and people select what they want or what their doctors have told them they need."

Life Lover's Lodge is not an elegant spa like LaCosta, or The Greenhouse, or Main Chance or some of the other luxurious pamper resorts, but it attracts its share of celebrities and the well to-do. Profits this year should hit $60,000.

Residential facilities such as diet, health and relaxation resorts can be immensely profitable. Unless they are managed carefully, however, they can be rapid and serious failures. The secrets of success in this business can be best expressed in the 3 C formula:

1. Continuous, creative market research and development so that advertising and promotion can be effectively pinpointed.

2. Careful catering to the needs and expectations of the customer-guest.
3. Conscientious control of every aspect of cost.

Dana and Charles control their labor costs, for example, in three ways. They do everything they can by themselves. That includes most of the maintenance, office work, and guest programs. For kitchen, food service, housekeeping and gardening, they offer scholarships or free stays to people who will work at assigned tasks. They also weave some of the necessary work into the guest program. Guests who have special interests in health, parapsychic, or awareness fields are asked to lead group discussions. Guests are also encouraged to work in the gardens which, from early summer to late fall, provide an abundance of raw foods for the spa.

YOU CAN JOIN THE CHARMED CIRCLE

The search for new ways to preserve the glow of health, youth and beauty has created many fortunes. As you apply the principles of *How to Get Rich Through OPN,* you may join the charmed circle that includes such famous names as Helena Rubinstein, Elizabeth Arden, The Revson-Revlon family and a host of others.

MINING THE GOLD IN THE GOLDEN YEAR MARKET

The years after children are grown and business or job responsibilities are reduced or eliminated entirely are sometimes called the golden years. For many people these years begin at 55 or 60 and meld into the senior years which are generally accepted to begin at 65.

Throughout this book there have been examples of how enterprising men and women have profitably filled some of the needs of this market. Lee C. specialized in job counseling for the older woman. Joey Y's classes in hypnotism served to fill leisure time and develop part-time income for retirees. Lila E and Claude R. have profited from older singles and the widowed or divorced. Manny B. is becoming a millionaire with his long-term hotel for seniors.

The golden year-senior market has numerous needs in common with other groups in our population, but it has many others which are distinct.

Senior citizens need to live as fully as possible, to enjoy the fruits of a lifetime of labor, to do the things there was no time for earlier, to defy aging by keeping as active as possible — these are psychological needs that characterize many in this market. The need of doting grandparents to jump the generation gap may be psychological, too, but it should be remembered that psychological needs produce tangible opportunities.

ANNIE DOTES ON DOTING GRANDMAS

Annie S. found one such opportunity when, on her doctor's orders, she moved west to a warm, dry climate to try to relieve her asthma attacks. Too weak to work at a full time job, Annie tried to develop a service she could sell to the many senior citizens who had come west to avoid the snow. Annie came up with a winner with her *Letters from a Covered Wagon.*

For $5, Annie offered to write a series of six two-page letters to "your favorite youngsters."

Her classified ad read:

> *Letters from A Covered Wagon* will teach
> your favorite youngsters the real rich history of
> the old west. A 2 page personalized letter every
> 10 days for 60 days. Send $5 with child's name,
> address and age. Different letters sent to mem-
> bers of same family.

Using a local library for research, Annie developed several series of letters written as though she were crossing the country with her family in the covered wagon days. When the demand was light, four or five letters a day — she wrote them long-hand. As the orders increased she had a printer offset her handwritten series using an ink she could match to fill in personal names. To keep the letters going out in proper order and at the right time, a series of six is addressed as soon as the order is received. The first letter is mailed and the others are placed in a date tickler file which is checked each day.

Responses to Annie's advertising ran from four most days to twenty at the height of the tourist season. Her expenses for advertising, postage and printing averaged $1.10 per order. When she was convinced that she had a money-maker, Annie began placing ads in other areas with a heavy golden age traffic. Today, she receives an average of 85 orders a day and employs a high school student to help personalize her letters from a covered wagon.

ONE'S COMPANY MULTIPLIES MONEY FROM MEALS

Sophie and Sam P. read an article that said many senior citizens who lived alone showed signs of malnutrition, not necessarily because of lack of friends but rather because of lack of motivation to prepare balanced meals. While some communities have developed a voluntary nonprofit Meals On Wheels program which delivers one hot meal a day, free or at nominal cost, no such program existed in their area, Sophie found out on a visit to the local Office for the Aging. A community meal program was sponsored by the agency, she was told, but it was offered in a school cafeteria and many seniors didn't take advantage of it because of special diet restrictions, inability to get out, and the (mistaken) notion that it was "charity."

Sophie and Sam carefully studied the statistics they secured from the agency. These included the number of people over 65, the numbers living alone, and the numbers at various income levels.

They checked with social service agencies and area physicians to get a subjective evaluation of their proposed new business. From the dietician at the city hospital they secured an assortment of menus for special diet requirements of people with high blood pressure, diabetes, and wheat, milk or egg allergies. Then, they began some test runs to establish basic costs.

"We determined that in addition to providing a well balanced meal we would rely on main dishes that were generally impractical to cook for one person — roast beef or turkey for example, and casseroles or ethnic dishes like stuffed cabbage, blintzes, kugels, etc. We found we could prepare a wholesome soup, salad, main dish, vegetable and dessert for an average of $2.20 per meal at retail prices, about 15% less if we bought in wholesale quantities. We had no idea what delivery would cost. We were planning to use our car to begin with, but we added $1 for transportation, disposable dishes and containers and part-time help. We decided arbitrarily that we'd charge $5 per meal delivered with a 25¢ discount per meal if there was an order for at least 5 meals per week. We thought it would be worthwhile for us if we could sell an average of 50 meals a day."

"It's not difficult to prepare 50 meals a day if you have the proper equipment. At a restaurant supply house we got a lead on a used range, freezer, refrigerator, pots and a meat slicer and salad maker, for $1,200. We decided to test the waters before we committed oursleves.

Ads in the weekly pennysaver and in the daily newspaper started a trickle of 5 or 6 orders a day. "It was like cooking for company," Sophie says. "We averaged about $8 a day profit. We were ready to give the whole thing up when we realized we were selling to the wrong people. The old people, even those who had money, were very frugal. They were terrified their money wouldn't last. That was part of the reason why they weren't eating well to begin with.

"Then we printed a leaflet and distributed it not only to doctors, hospital discharge offices, and social service agencies, but also to rabbis, priests and ministers who we thought might suggest our service to congregants.

That's when business started booming. The old people still weren't ordering in great numbers but their sons and daughters and in-laws were placing orders for them.

Sam believes the service helps these grown and married children erase some of their guilt feelings about their responsibilities to aging parents living in separate households. In some instances, he says, several children share in the weekly costs.

You can learn from Sam and Sophie that the market is not only where the money is but also where the motivation exists for spending the money. You can also learn that guilt feelings make a mighty powerful motivation.

MAKING AN INCOME WITH MA BELL

Alyse J., a shut-in herself, earns her keep helping oldsters fill the need for human contact. For $18 a month she calls once a day for a 3 to 5 minute chat in which she reminds them to take their medicines, keep their doctor's appointments and pay their bills. When people subscribe to her service, or their children subscribe for them, Alyse fills out a card with all the pertinent information. Additional notes are added as she talks to the subscriber. She makes about 40 calls a day.

"Lots of old people are afraid to go out of their apartments nowadays" Alyse says. They're also afraid that they'll get sick or die and no one will know." Her subscribers are asked to tell her in advance if they will be out for any reason. Alyse calls around the same time each day. If they don't answer, Alyse calls back in 15 minutes. After the second no answer call, Alyse calls the building super, a neighbor, or the nearest police station and asks them to check.

"Mostly its a false alarm, but we've found a few people who've had strokes and two who had been tied up by burglars, so it pays to follow up. I get so involved with these people they seem like family and I worry about all of them. But it makes me feel good to be able to help and the $600 or $800 I earn every month pays my way."

HOW ELWOOD R. FOUND SECURITY

No matter how he tried, Elwood R. couldn't keep ahead of the bills on his salary as a gas station attendant. Worse than that, he was scared. The station had been broken into twice. Elwood was sure it was just a matter of time till someone would stage a robbery when he was on duty. As he leafed through one of the salesmen's opportunity magazines he saw several ads for security systems and personal safety devices. He wrote for information on several different kinds of alarms, door locks, one-way viewers, a personal whistle, and a defend-yourself-spray. He borrowed $100 from his boss for some salesmen's samples. Every day after work he knocked at doors in areas where the aged population predominated. In ten days he handed the $100 back to his boss. Two weeks later he handed in his notice. He was making twice his salary in his spare time and he wanted to be his own boss.

TILLIE'S TOURS SAVE HOTEL FROM AUCTION BLOCK

Aaron H. and his family had run a small hotel for 40 years. To keep up with competition Aaron invested in a modernization program financed by a large mortgage. Shortly thereafter, the foreign travel boom began and Aaron's market dwindled.

"We had always looked askance at our older guests," Aaron recalls, "because we thought they discouraged younger people from coming. Suddenly the senior citizens were our mainstay and we weren't getting enough of them. We found, though, that we could cut our costs considerably catering to this market. They ate less, required less costly entertainment and fewer athletic facilities.

Aaron began to research the senior market systematically. His advertising agent prepared lists of publications with heavy senior readership. "But advertising was too expensive," he recalls. "We got a few of our guests to represent us in their apartment buildings, giving them about 10% in cash or vacations. We still weren't doing well enough to pay our mortgage amortization. We were sure we'd lose the place. Then Tillie D. asked if we'd give her Senior Circle Club a discount. They wanted to come on Monday for dinner and stay until after lunch Tuesday. The place was going to be empty and we had to pay the staff, so we quoted Tillie a group rate about 20% less than our regular price and we promised her 5%. We were happy to give her $80. She also made $20 on the two buses."

It was satisfactory all around. Tillie went back to the city and solicited other senior citizens groups. "She brings in two or three tours a month" Aaron says. "We get a lot of private business from people who come back after a tour. We've become an older crowd hotel. We should have done it years ago."

Tillie secures lists of senior citizen clubs through the Office for the Aging in her state. She also purchases lists of retired people from a mailing list company. She works with the charter division of a bus company to arrange transportation for the tours she packages.

"The most important success factor in handling senior citizens groups," she says, "is attention to details. If you schedule lunch at noon, you have to see that it's served at 12 sharp. You have to stick with the outlined schedule or have a compelling reason not to. You also have to be able to cope with emergencies and know how to make arrangements for the occasional episode of illness, including a heart attack. I keep a list of hospitals along any route we take. The objective is to see that the victim is taken care of as adequately and quickly as possible and to disrupt the rest of the group as little as possible."

SEVEN SERVICES FOR SENIORS

A tally of *your* talents will tell you how to trade them for treasures in the senior market. You may find the key in one of the successful services below:

Counseling the Dying: Nettie P. took a course in thanatology, the study of death and dying, and now serves as a consultant to hospitals and nursing homes teaching personnel how to deal with terminal patients and their families. In some areas counselors can now be retained on an individual basis to help a terminal patient face the inevitable.

Taping After-Death Instructions: Meyer N. charges $50 an hour to record 15 to 20 minute taped messages and instructions for attorneys, next-of-kin, and others named as executors who will administer estates. The taping fee includes two copies. Additional copies are charged at $10 each. Tape boxes are sealed, dated and witnessed. Meyer urges clients to have a written will prepared by an attorney. In business only a short time, Meyer's handling an average of six clients a month.

Senior Sitting: Betsy K. switched from baby sitting to senior sitting when she discovered how many families had problems caring for senile parents who could not be left alone. At $4 an hour, plus meals and trasportation, Betsy's schedule is full.

Driving: For northern vacationers who want their cars in Florida but prefer to fly themselves, Dan H. drives the auto for $35 a day plus meals, motel and auto expenses and airfare back.

Teaching Self Defense: Sari N. learned the secrets of judo and karate and now teaches the arts of self defense to senior citizens.

Oldsters pay $4 each for group lessons, $10 for private lessons. Sari runs 6 group classes a week at a community center which offers the course as a public service.

Selling Life Income: Jack S. recognized in the golden year market a great need for financial security. He sought out an insurance company which would train him and now nets over $50,000 a year selling annuities.

Selling Retirement Homes: Armand L. read the real estate section of the Sunday papers and noted the large number of promotions geared to the potential retirement home buyer. He contacted four developments in different parts of the country and became their area representative. His commissions on the 30 to 40 homes he sells each year has solved his financial problems now and enabled him to acquire a retirement home for his old age.

13

BUILDING BLOCKS TO BETTER INCOMES FILLING HOMEOWNERS' NEEDS

A FIRST CLASS INCOME
IN A SECOND HOME DEVELOPMENT

Kelly S. moved his family from their city apartment to a house in the country so quickly he didn't stop to think how he'd make a living there. "Our daughter had been beaten in a school hallway," he says. "There wasn't any way I'd let her go back to that jungle even if I had to commute to work every day. Houses in the sub- urbs were too high priced for us so we kept looking farther away until we bought a place in a development about 70 miles from the city. It was a quiet town with no industry, but it was the center of a popular hunting and fishing area."

Kelly couldn't find work in the country. To keep the family going, he returned to his old job, commuting nearly three hours a day. "It was terrible," Kelly recalls, "and it was expensive. The house was also costing more than we anticipated. It had been built for price I guess, and at four years of age it needed a lot of work. I was lucky. I could handle the problems myself. Most of our neighbors had bought second homes for vacations or to retire to. They were constantly shelling out money."

When a neighbor told Kelly that he had gotten an $800 estimate for painting the outside of his house, Kelly offered to do it for $450 plus the cost of paint.

The job took four weekends rather than the three Kelly had figured it would. Despite that and although he had spent some money on brushes and rollers, paint scrapers, drop cloths, and rental of an extension ladder, Kelly wound up with over $5 an hour. That was more than he cleared on his commuting job.

He didn't dare give up his job, though, until he was sure he could pick up a steady income housepainting. He left hand-lettered cards at the paint store and tacked up small posters at the supermarket. In a month he had lined up five jobs and enough confidence to become a full-time painting contractor.

Kelly used his first experience as a guide for estimating, though he quickly recognized the time-consuming spots. Now he measures the house and counts doors, windows, shutters and other areas which might require special attention. "There's still no formula, he says. "I estimate the number of hours at $6.50 an hour and add on about 10% as a cushion. If business is slow, I can play around with the cushion, but I don't usually have to."

When Kelly adds up his expenses for telephone, advertising, insurance, salaries and employment taxes and automobiles, he finds he's clearing $24,000 a year on his own labor and that of 6 part-time employees. "We've expanded out of the area, "Kelly points out, "and in addition to house painting inside and out, we do offices, hotels and public buildings. That second home development started us on a first class income!"

ANALYZING THE HOMEOWNER'S MARKET

There are three major classifications of homeowners. They are owners of:

1. A primary home
2. A second-home
3. A retirement home

Kelly's flight from the city is typical of hundreds of thousands who move to a primary home in the suburbs or country to escape the changing environment of their neighborhoods. While some of these people own their homes in the city, the vast majority are apartment dwellers who have had no experience with home ownership. Nevertheless, because zoning restrictions in many non-urban areas preclude or limit multiple dwellings, most people who want to live in such areas must become homeowners.

There are also those who have selected to live in private homes as status symbols, or to accommodate large families, or for various other personal reasons.

No matter what their reasons, those people who establish their residence in a home of their own fall into the category of primary home owners. As a rule, the primary homes do not change ownership as frequently as second homes, receive a larger portion of the owner's income and form a larger part of the market.

Second homes might better be called secondary homes because they are dwellings owned and used in addition to the primary home or apartment. For most people, second homes are weekend, holiday and seasonal retreats. Some people have more than one second home. Such homes are usually located in country areas, along the seashore, around lakes and rivers, in the mountains or other areas offering recreational or cultural attractions.

Owners of second homes generally have higher than average incomes, and though they characteristically have more leisure time, they are not necessarily "do-it-yourselfers."

Second homes during the income-producing years may become retirment homes when the working years are over, and retirement homes usually become primary homes. For many people in the retirement market the motivations include the search for healthful climates, costs to meet the limitations of their fixed incomes and the desire to live in compatible communities.

It is wise to remember these distinctions when "imaginating" the homeowners' market because each category opens new doors to profits. You should keep in mind that the number of new homes built each year is a reflection of the state of the economy and the money market. As one of the economic indicators, housing starts reported periodically by the Department of Commerce can give you a green light or a caution signal for many business ventures. New furniture sales, for instance are highly dependent on new housing starts, just as used furnishing sales increase in a sluggish economy.

In your own area you can identify new developments or housing projects in the real estate sections of your newspapers. You can also secure names of homeowners from your County Clerk's office where deeds are recorded. These are public records and you can view them without charge. You can also learn of transfers of property, mortgages, liens, collateral loans and other financial transactions which have been publicly recorded by subscribing to a legal or business service which serves your area.

The availability of this information makes the homeowners' market a well defined and easily identifiable target for sales efforts.

Ellsworth and Edith J. earned a fantastic 3200% return on a $250 investment by catering to the do-it-yourself market in their busy suburban area with many moderately priced tract houses. Using their garage as a base they spent their money advertising a tool registry co-op. For an annual fee of $6 members can list their tools and receive a quarterly listing of other members' equipment and the rental fees. Members are given code numbers and bring their equipment to the "co-op" when Edith advises them that there is a call for it. Ellsworth and Edith were able to sign up over 500 members — some of them from as much as 25 miles away — in less than a year. Each member, they found, spent an average of $90 a year on rentals. With minimal expenses for insurance, advertising, phone and mimeographed mailings, Edith and Ellsworth's first year profit was $8,000.

Albert T. makes a living repairing lawn mowers, snow blowers and roto-tillers, while Burt L. earns his servicing dishwashers, washing machines, dryers, disposals and other major appliances. Moira deJ. turned her talents for stitching into a profitable business selling custom made draperies, slip covers and bedspreads.

Nancy W. became wealthy as an interior decorator for stylish suburban homes.

Sherman K. earns over $40,000 a year supervising crews who give a one-day household overhaul service. His fees, based on the size of the house, start at $100 a day and cover window cleaning, floor waxing, carpet cleaning, furniture waxing, tile cleaning, etc.

TWENTY-TWO NEEDS YOU CAN BANK ON

Homeowners have a multitude of needs which are creating new opportunities for you at this very moment. Some of them are:

1. Landscaping
2. Lawn Care
3. Leaf Removal
4. Tree Care
5. Gutter cleaning and Replacement
6. Sidewalk, Driveway and Patio Paving and Repair
7. Fencing and Screening for Privacy or Security
8. Snow Removal
9. Garbage Removal
10. Septic Tank Cleaning
11. Window, storm and screen cleaning and changing
12. Chimney Cleaning
13. Air conditioning
14. Heating
15. Plumbing
16. Carpentry
17. Electrician's Services
18. Roofing
19. Cellar, garage and attic cleaning
20. House — sitting or checking
21. House opening or closing
22. Exterminating

While not all of these services may be required in your particular area, they and others mentioned in this chapter will serve as take-off points for your own imagining. Nils O. started this way when he was fresh out of high school and he's been racking up the profits ever since.

RACKING UP PROFITS WITH ROCKS

Nils O. earns $2,000 a month from early spring to late fall because he recognized a need and developed a special way to fill it. Nils knew that the landscaping outfits in his area were coining money and even the teenagers with mowers were clearing $30 to $40 a day during summer vacations. "What an expense that must be for the homeowner," he thought, "thousands of dollars to put in a lawn to begin with, and hundreds of dollars every year to maintain it."

Nils began reading everything he could find on lawns, landscaping, and gardens, seeking a way to cut lawn maintenance and costs. His solution? Perennial rock gardens, pebble paths, and ground cover plantings. "Once these are planted, they require much less care than traditional lawns. They give a more casual, natural look which many homeowners want, particularly around country homes. They also solve the problem of what to do with a site that is hilly, uneven, rocky and without much topsoil."

Nils picks up some rocks and boulders at construction sites. He also accumulates quantities of stones and rocks along the banks of a river near his home. On occasion he has purchased special rocks from quarries all over the country. He buys his pebbles from a sand and gravel bank and his ground cover plants and most perennials from a wholesale nursery. His charges run $2 a square foot plus costs for rocks, pebbles and plants. "Often we use wild flowers already on the property, or we encourage homeowners to go plant-hunting in the woods."

Nils takes color slides of each of his jobs. He uses these to show to prospective customers during the winter. He advertises to new homeowners year round by direct mail, securing names from deeds recorded in the County Clerk's office. He also relies on ads in area newspapers during the pre-Christmas season. He works on a written contract, with 1/3 on signing, 1/3 when the job is started and the balance on satisfactory completion. The guarantee of satisfaction sometimes costs Nils some extra work, but he thinks its worth it to get recommendations.

PROFIT FROM A $2 LABEL MAKER

Helga E. was home alone when she heard the sound of water surging in her finished basement. A pipe had burst and the water was flooding the recreation room. The answering service told her they'd give the plumber the message, but in the meantime "close the valve from the water main or check to see if your sump pump switch is jammed." Helga didn't know a valve from a switch or a main from a left field. She was afraid to touch anything she wasn't sure of. Her plumbing bill came to $65, but it cost several hundred to repair the damage to the floor, furnishings and paneled walls of the recreation room.

It didn't make Helga feel any better to know that many of her neighbors had felt similarly helpless during home emergencies. Helga was determined that it would never happen to her again.

She called the plumber, the heating man and the electrician and paid each of them for a service call to identify the switches, buttons, valves, fuse boxes and controls in her basement and to explain how they should be pushed or turned in an emergency. Using an inexpensive labeling tape device, Helga labeled each unit with its name and a cryptic note such as *Up Is On* or *Push in to Reset*. She recorded the location of each unit on a master card which she hung at the head of the stairs.

"Just knowing what and where everything is, gave me confidence," Helga says. "It had the same effect on my best friend, when I labeled her house. She suggested that I make it a business."

Helga advertised in the classfieds offering to label other houses for $50. Her service people often recommend her services because it takes the pressure off them in emergencies. A development builder asked for and got a half rate package on 40 identical houses. In a year Helga earned over $7,500, working part time. She's added manila tags, fluorescent self-adhesive labels, and a mimeographed instruction booklet to her identification system. "Some day," she says, "I may just become a lady plumber."

CHECKING UNLIVED IN HOMES
BRINGS WILLIE STEADY CHECKS

Willie M. made a frugal living doing odd jobs for homeowners, but he never knew when the next job would pop up or how much income he could count on. Things were particularly rough in the winter. His steady customers took their vacations and the second-home people came up only on weekends and holidays. Most people waited for the spring for house projects. In the winter Willie was called chiefly for emergencies.

It was after one emergency call, that Willie saw the need for a special service for unlived in houses. He had been called to clean a week-end retreat in which the pipes had frozen and burst because the heating system stopped working. The owner was covered by insurance, but nothing could compensate for the mess and the inconvenience.

Willie suggested a warning device to the homeowner. "It has a red light that goes on when the temperature falls below a certain point," he said. When the homeowner asked who would see the light, Willie offered to check the house for 50¢ a day. He got $15 in advance for the first month. After arranging to buy the warning devices wholesale, he advertised his new product and services by mail to the homeowners for whom he had worked. On weekends, he went door to door selling. It wasn't long before he had made $500 on his sales and had 40 regulars on his route — $600 a month for his slow season simply because he was able to fill a need.

Bertha K. fills a need, too. She makes her money on short term rentals of homes when the owners aren't using them. Ads in the city real estate section bring her a lengthy list of people who will pay $100 a week for a vacation home which she rents from owners at $200 a month. Sure, the owners could do their renting on their own. That's where Bertha got her idea. But she discovered that many second-home owners didn't want to be bothered with weekly rentals. They preferred dealing with one responsible individual whom they could depend on.

Hollis G. nets $6,000 for 2 months work closing 60 summer homes for the winter and opening them for the spring. He drains the water systems so that frost won't cause the pipes to burst;

he shuts off all electrical switches and turns off appliances; and he boards up windows and doors so the buildings cannot be used by transients. In the spring he reverses the project.

Marilou I., a young mother of three, was determined to support herself and her children even though their father had left them. When she tabulated her skills and talents she couldn't match them with any needs of the homeowners market until she gained a new perspective. Her new view set her up in a stimulating profitable business. It may do the same for you.

MARILOU'S HOWDY NEIGHBOR SERVICE

Marilou didn't view her gift of gab as an asset — it always got her into trouble — until she realized she was spending most of her time telling new neighbors whom to call for what service and where to buy what they needed. Obviously newcomers had a need to know this information. How could she fill this need profitably? Marilou listed these ideas.

1. A shopping guide or pennysaver paper that could be published weekly.
2. A directory of stores and services.
3. A telephone information service.
4. A personal introductory tour.

Marilou knew she could talk merchants into advertising in a guide or directory, but she had little business experience and was afraid to tackle ideas 1 and 2. She knew she could handle ideas 3 and 4, but she didn't know if she could reach enough newcomers who would pay for the service.

It was while she was imagining this problem that she suddenly realized that merchants and service people had a greater need to reach the new owners than vice-versa. More than that she knew that homeowners usually continued dealing with the merchants and tradesmen they started with.

"How much would you pay to have your business personally introduced to the 30 to 40 new homeowners who come into an area each month?" Marilou asked the service people and merchants with whom she did business. She found the majority willing to make a commitment of $1 per homeowner if she agreed to represent only one business or service of each type. It took her less than 2 weeks to line up a bank, a dairy, a fuel oil company, a drug store, an upholsterer, a hardware store, a children's shop, an Italian restaurant, a bakery and a women's specialty shop along with her plumber, electrician, painter and carpenter.

Each subscriber gives Marilou some business cards, advertising flyers, introductory offers to new customers such as cents-off coupons or special rates for an initial purchase; an invitation to receive a free gift or service if they visit or call; free samples, or inexpensive useful gifts. Marilou packages these with any available civic literature available from area agencies and service clubs. She uses a drawstring type plastic bag which she buys from a paper supply house.

She gets her names of new owners from property transfer records and gives each merchant a list for mailings. The average visit takes twenty minutes. "If no one is home after three visits, I leave the bag with the drawstring hung on a doorknob with a note giving my number," Marilou says. "Traveling time takes an average of 15 minutes per call. I usually represent about 25 establishments so I'm getting $25 for 35 minutes work. People move in and out of the area all the time even when building is slow. I average $650 a month from this and I've been able to pick up another $350 a month working part-time in one of the shops I represent."

To be successful in a business like Marilou's requires an area with a sufficient turnover of property or new home sales. You can investigate this potential by checking the records for previous transfers and by talking to area bankers who are familiar with new development potential.

ANOTHER HALF-DOZEN HOMEOWNERS' NEEDS

1. Adam R., a free-lance writer, earns up to $100 a week and lives rent-free in some of the nicest homes in the country. Adam became a house sitter when he discovered that many people do not like to leave their homes unattended while they are on vacation or away on business. Ads in literary magazines got Adam started on this extra income opportunity which takes him all over the country. Responsibilities include making sure that house emergencies are handled by calling professionals whose names are left by the owners, answering phones, caring for pets, plants, etc.

2. Channing S., an out-of-work television cameraman, now earns approximately $75 an hour videotaping home inventories for insurance records in case of loss. Chan originally rented his camera, later bought a used one for under $200. He photographs every room in the house so that all furnishings are shown, takes close-ups of closet interiors, drawers, and other areas where insured possessions are stored. Homeowners get the original videotape which they are advised to keep in a bank safe deposit box.

3. Harry P. became a rich man with a door to door route buying furnishings housewives wanted to dispose of for cash. Starting with $200 in cash and an old pick-up truck, Harry made it a point never to pay more than 25% of what he thought he could sell an item for. Moving from neighborhood to neighborhood, he often sold the item not long after he bought it. Unsold items were taken to his home where he eventually built a quonset hut. The secret of making lots of money at anything, Harry knew, is to turn over your capital as frequently as possible, each time making a profit. In order to accomplish this, he began weekly auctions to dispose of his own accumulations and to handle complete household dispersal sales at a commission ranging from 15% to 33-1/3%.

4. Esther G. also capitalized on peddler profits with a door to door route through tract developments. Esther sold color coordinated linens — sheets, pillow-cases, blanket covers, bedspreads, draperies, towels and bathroom accessories which she bought from a wholesaler. Esther, who secures a peddler's license from each community she sells in, covers each area once every six weeks. Working an average of 3 days a week she clears over $18,000 yearly. "Many women like the idea of being able to see color matches in their own home before they buy," Esther says. While she occasionally handles discount job lots, most of her prices are geared to those in department stores.

5. Kelsey L. invested less than $100 in woodburning equipment and a sabre-saw and makes his investment back every day he sells woodburned name signs to homeowners at fairs and flea markets. Kelsey's prices start at $8.50 for a 6" x 18" sign which says "The Your Names Live Here." Blanks are cut from 3/4" pine; lettered while the customer waits or shops and protected by a quick-drying oil stain. On vacations, Kelsey sells to campers. He also places mail order ads in the pre-Christmas season, starting in September.

6. Pearl and Victor R. buy distressed houses at low prices, with the lowest possible down payments, provide attractive cosmetic finishes doing most of the work themselves, and resell at a profit as quickly as possible. Their purchases have ranged from $12,000 to $22,000. Improvements are generally those which "show" the most: fresh white paint, the addition of closets, repair or replacement of obvious sales-spoilers like light bulbs handing on electric cords; inexpensive neutral carpeting throughout; single walls of paneling, mirror, cork or some other dramatic effect-material. Average cost of improvements with any additional labor needed has been $1200. Last year they bought, refinished, and sold 8 houses with a net profit of $32,000. In addition, one of their properties came on three acres of land. When they sold it, they kept two acres and a right of way to be sold at a later date. "Land prices are going up, says Victor. "As long as the taxes don't go up too high, we'll keep it as a reserve."

14

GOING INTO THE NEED FULFILLING BUSINESS

A NOTEWORTHY NAME CAN SPREAD YOUR FAME

You've discovered a need, developed a service or product to fill that need and determined that you're ready to reap the rewards of your own business. Before you make your first public announcement you will want to consider your business name. Choosing a name is an important decision. Major corporations often spend hundreds of thousands of dollars to create names for their operations or for individual products and services; then, they invest additional sums to advertise the names they have chosen.

Some of the factors they consider are·

1. Is the name original? Is anyone else using the same or similar name?

2. Does the name provide an instant identification of the product(s) or service(s) handled?

3. Does the name allow for growth, change or diversification?

4. Are there any "image" connotations to the name, and if so, are these images favorable?

5. Is the name short and simple enough to use on letterheads, business cards, etc., and in advertising?

6. Is the name easy to remember?

If you are going to be an incorporated business, the Secretary of State office in your state will generally not issue corporation papers if the name you propose is the same or very similar to another corporation in the state. If you are not incorporating your business most states require that you file a business certificate at your county clerk's office. These certificates are public records and indicate so called d/b/a or "doing business as" assumed names. You can check them to see the names other businessmen and women have used.

You can secure information on registering your business or product name nationally from the U.S. Copyright Office, Washington, D.C.

The name you choose can bring you fortune in cost-free advertising. The person who opened a pawn shop and called it "The Happy Hocker" received a wealth of publicity. So did the people who christened their Christmas tree farm "Love and XX-mas Trees." Gary Dahl is reputed to have cleared a cool million selling ordinary run-of-the-mountain stones to several hundred thousand who paid $3.95 for a "Pet Rock." His farm is called Rock Bottom Productions. Joshua Reynolds capitalized on current interest in self-awareness when he developed an encapsulated substance which changed colors while it was being held — and called it a "Mood Stone." One bedding store labels its products "Rex Rated"; Another calls itself "Sleepworld"; still another in a popular racetrack area bears the sign "Off-track Bedding."

It's easy to come up with noteworthy names if you learn a few word tricks.

HOW TO COIN A NAME

Coining new words or combinations is the key to creating clever names. There are several techniques in this process. One is to create a sound-alike. Another is to change a letter or syllable in a familiar word, or substitute an unexpected word as a prefix or suffix. You can also coin words by taking off on a well known word or phrase — rhyming, punning, or combining ordinary words in unusual ways.

Let's take some examples: a children's barber shop is called "Heir Cuts; a gourmet cooking school is named "The Happy Cooker," a restaurant specializing in omelets calls itself "Egg-cetera," a book store catering to mystery readers is named "Murder, Ink"; "Feasts To Go" is a home catering business; another is called "A Moveable Feast." Pies are sold in "Jack Horner's Corner." A deli selling take home soups is "The Souperstar." Thrift shops have been named "New to You," Second Time Around," and "Use for Yous."

You can start yourself on the name creation process by making a list of synonyms or popular words or phrases for your product or service, for the things or people it works on or for, for the benefits it offers, the popular characters — real or fictional whose attributes are applicable and any descriptive words which pertain to it.

If you're going into a commercial house cleaning service, for example, your list might look like this:

house	scrub	glow
home	neat as a pin	sparkle
apartment	clean as a whistle	Sparkle Plenty
pad	squeaky clean	bright
lair	less work for	attractive
castle	homemaker	quick
chalet	fresh as a daisy	fast
home is where	cleanliness is	easy
the heart is	next to godliness	simple
home on the range	mother-in-law	inexpensive
your home is your	approval	dependable
castle	under the rug clean	thorough
cabin in the sky	compliments	complete
		compleat

From the above list you might arrive at such names as *Sparkle Plenty Housecleaners; Compliments for the House; The Compleat Cleaner, The Goodly Cleaners; The Whistle Cleaners; Pad Perkers; Mother-In-Law Approved Cleaners; Glow Glow Girls,* etc.

KEEPING RECORDS FOR YOURSELF AND UNCLE SAM

Keeping account records can help you legally cut your income taxes to the lowest possible point. It is important, therefore, to keep not only cancelled checks, but also sales slips, receipts and invoices for all of your business expenditures and a written record of all cash expenditures you make for your business. In many instances, you will also be able to include as expenses, some costs of your home if it is used for business, your car, your telephone, etc. It is important to remember, however, that revisions and new interpretations of the tax laws are made periodically. They should be checked before deductions are taken.

To learn how to set up your records, you can contact the Small Business Administration and your State Department of Commerce for various booklets on bookkeeping and record keeping. Be sure to indicate what kind of business you will be operating, since some booklets are specifically geared to certain fields. It is wise, too, to include as an initial and periodic expense, the professional advice of an accountant who can show you how to handle specific aspects of your record keeping for all of the tax forms required by city, state and federal agencies.

LOW COST — NO COST WAYS TO PROMOTE BUSINESS

1. Have post card size cards printed carrying the message "I just tried _____ and I think you'd like it." Or some similar copy recommending your product or service. Affix proper postage and ask your customer to sign the message and send cards to their friends.

2. Regularly send news releases and photos to newspapers and radio and television stations in your marketing areas(s). Subjects can include announcements of opening or special events; unusual products or services; in-

    struction on how-to-make or do something; unusual autobiographical material; unusual orders filled; insight into human nature, marketing or sales, etc.; famous customers (with their permission); etc.

3. Develop a *free expert* service for radio and television stations and/or newspapers. Write a regular column or tape a brief program about your field with tips to readers, viewers and listeners. Do not commercialize your material with reference to your particular business but offer to answer questions which are sent in.

4. Keep your notices posted on bulletin boards, whenever permitted, in shopping centers, schools, offices, hospitals, centers, etc.

5. Sell by telephone. Develop a brief telephone questionnaire or sales pitch and make a fixed number of calls each day to develop interest, pick up leads, or to make actual sales.

HOW TO PIGGY BACK YOUR PROFITS

You can piggy-back your profits by adding allied products or services to your business. Gennine R started with leather crafted pocketbooks and added belts, plant-holders, wall-hangings, game boards, and furniture tops. Mendel S. added a line of homemade jellies and jams to his traveling produce van. Glenda T. started selling silk-screened stationery and piggy-backed a line of greeting cards, mini-posters and bar signs. Bennie U. sold stationery products to businesses. He tripled his income when he became a representative for a used business machine and office furniture company.

The examples above represent a *diversification of products within the same market.*

You can also piggy back profits by *diversifying your markets for the same products or services.* Harry O. averaged $6 an hour snow plowing driveways in a development. He doubled that when he added shopping centers to his market. Kay N. sold her services as a free lance interior decorator to furniture stores as well as to homemakers. Lorretta S. started selling patchwork pillows at craft fairs and diversified her market to include antique shops and department stores. Ralph G. who carved Colonial reproductions for an area antique shop found himself with more orders than he could handle when he placed a mail order ad in a national home magazine.

You can piggy back your profits, too, by combining forces with others. Painters, plumbers, carpenters, electricians, decorators, etc., can increase their earnings by associations with architects and contractors. Teachers and lecturers in allied fields can multiply their individual incomes by developing seminar programs. People who sell direct mail can often cut their mailing costs and consequently reach larger markets by combining their mailings with others offering non-competitive products.

If you have developed a profitable market, look for others whose products or services are also needed in that market. Organize a registry service or take your referral commissions individually, or contract for their products or services at a fixed rate and take your profits from your markets. Of course, you can also profit from those you hire as employees. Where it is possible to have people work for you as independent contractors rather than employees, the former route is preferable. If you do have the employees, however, it is important to add to your labor expense the "hidden costs" of insurance, payroll taxes and record keeping and inevitable periods of unproductive time.

HOW TO SUCCEED IN THE NEED FULFILLMENT BUSINESS

1. Start with a need which exists in a Sufficient number of people to create a Substantial market for a Serious Sales Spur.

2. Use your self assessment chart to Uncover a talent, skill, or Understanding you can Utilize to develop a product or service to fill that need.

3. Cash in on Crises, Crazes and uncommon Circumstances which offer quick Chances to Clean-Up with a Clever product or service.

4. Check and re-check your Costs and Control all expenditures which do not Contribute to Profits.

5. Emulate the successes of others and Embrace success as

a friend you deserve to meet Every day in Each Effort you make.

6. <u>S</u>ell yourself along with your product or Service and Say "Yes" to the profitable Sidelines which will unfold before you.

7. <u>S</u>ail every Sea, calm or rough, with the confidence that you will ride out each storm because *you deserve Success.*

Index